NATIONAL IDENTITY IN THE BRITISH ISLES.

Edited by

NEIL EVANS

Coleg Harlech Occasional Papers in Welsh Studies No. 3.

1989

CONTENTS

Preface

With two exceptions, the papers collected here were presented at a Welsh Studies Dayschool held at Coleg Harlech on 23rd April- St. George's Day-1988. I cannot say honestly that the timing was deliberate! Like most people in the British Isles, I am rarely conscious of the significamce of that day. The two papers which did not originate at the dayschool are my introductory essay, which was written subsequently, and John Osmond's contribution which was presented to the Conference of Extra-Mural Tutors in Wales on 'New Directions' at Cardiff in July 1988. As it fitted so well with the themes of this paper I was delighted when he agreed to include it in this publication. Apart from the introduction all the essays remain essentially in the form of spoken contributions. The introduction aims to provide a broad framework for the essays that follow by approaching some of the key debates on the British state and the nationalities that have co-existed in these islands.

This publication has a limited length and started from a desire to place the experience of Wales in a wider perspective. This accounts for what some might see as its undue emphasis on the Welsh experience, and its omission of any sustained discussion of the 26 counties of Ireland or of Scotland. Both areas figure to some extent in the pages that follow, and neither the dayschool nor this occasional paper exhaust the interest of Coleg Harlech in the general topic. We hope our friends in Scotland and the Republic of Ireland will forgive their absence on this occasion.

I would like to thank all the contributors for their promptness in delivering their scripts, and apologise to them for being slower than I intended in doing the editing and production work. Mena Ifans's help, good sense and experience was vital in that process. Paul Edwards of the Industrial Relations Research Unit, University of Warwick and David Henderson also gave important help in that sphere. Harvey Cox, Bernard Crick and Ieuan Gwynedd Jones gave me very helpful comments on the introduction which I have tried to act upon. They, Emyr Williams and

3

John Osmond also encouraged me in my rashness, but, of course, bear no responsibility for the outcome. Joe England suggested the idea of publishing the contributions in the first place and has encouraged and supported me in the work.

The views expressed in the various contributions are those of the authors and not of Coleg Harlech, which has no corporate view. As in all our publications we offer this as a contribution to the free debate that is vital to democratic politics and to a healthy and vigorous culture.

Neil Evans.   14 July 1989

Contributors

Harvey Cox is Lecturer in Political Theory and Institutions at the University of Liverpool. His publications include, *Cities: The Public Dimension*, (1976) and a series of articles on Irish politics in the journal, *Parliamentary Affairs*.

Bernard Crick is Emeritus Professor of Politics at Birkbeck College, University of London. His many publications include, *In Defence of Politics*, (1962); *George Orwell: A Life*, (1981); and *Socialism*, (1987)

Neil Evans is Tutor in History and Welsh Studies at Coleg Harlech. He has published a number of articles and reviews on modern Welsh and British History

John Osmond is Assistant Editor of *Wales on Sunday*, having worked previously for the *Yorkshire Evening Post*, the *Western Mail*, and *Arcade* as well as for HTV. He has published widely on contemporary politics, including, *Creative Conflict*, (1977) and *The Divided Kingdom*, (1988)

Emyr Williams is Cooperative Development and Training Officer for South Gwynedd with the Wales Cooperative Agency. He completed a thesis on the early history of Plaid Cymru at the University College of Wales, Aberystwyth, and has been a temporary tutor at Coleg Harlech. A prominent figure in the Plaid Cymru National Left, he has published numerous articles in English and in Welsh.

INTRODUCTION
IDENTITY AND INTEGRATION IN THE BRITISH ISLES

NEIL EVANS

> The national identities of the people of the United Kingdom are multiple, not singular. Few people will feel equally at home in London, Edinburgh, Cardiff and Belfast. Anyone who did so would seem rootless rather than rooted in a British identity. Nor could such a person claim to be cosmopolitan, for some of these are considered provincial centres. (Richard Rose)

This approach to the United Kingdom has become a more common one in the past decade. In the sixties there seemed to be a single entity called Britain and textbooks in a variety of disciplines extolled its relative homogeneity. The point of reference for this argument was frequently the United States. On one occasion, at an international conference, Harold Wilson objected to his being seated as the representative of the United Kingdom and insisted that he represented Britain. It has become notorious that to study these islands (to use one of the least contentious terms!) is to step into a minefield of nomenclature. Few return unscathed. 'Britain' (for instance in some series of history textbooks) often means 'Greater England'. However, the problem is beginning to be recognised and recently Keith Robbins, Edward Royle and John Stevenson have produced volumes which are genuinely about Britain. In political science things seem to have gone further. Richard Rose in the work quoted in the epigraph has produced one attempt at a general synthesis of the working of the system, and Jim Bulpitt's more historically inclined (but also theoretically rooted) study is challenging and provocative. Rose has gone so far as to turn the old homogeneity on its head and to proclaim that the U.K. is a multinational state. That Habsburg resonance is perhaps something that ought to cause us to pause to think. Tom Nairn and Neal Ascherson also refer to it in their recent work. What is the nature of this entity that we find difficult even to name confidently?

The answer is clearly not a simple one. The two large offshore European Islands were a single political entity only for the 121 years of the Irish Union, yet the histories of the peoples who inhabited them have

6

interacted for much longer and continue to do so. The most positive feature of the Anglo (sic)-Irish Agreement is its recognition of that elementary fact. But is this agglomeration really a multinational kingdom if measured on the Habsburg or Romanov scale? It would be a difficult case to sustain. England's dominance has been of such long-standing and its numerical preponderance usually so overwhelming that little could stand in its path. By the standards of a multinational kingdom, the centre was immensely powerful, and it had a limited territory to overwhelm. Rose himself makes the telling point that the logical centre for a kingdom based on the British Isles would be Liverpool. London's continual orientation towards the continent of Europe is indicative of other priorities and these have skewed the whole development in particular ways. The states which emerged earliest on the Atlantic seaboard- France, Spain and England/ Britain- were amongst those that were least tolerant of ethnic and linguistic diversity. The centre's chances of overwhelming the periphery seemed good and stability seemed to require it. The multinational empires of central and eastern Europe, however, faced a more complex situation. In the Habsburg Empire in 1780 there were eleven major nationalities, not to mention the more fragmentary peoples. Not one of them constituted a majority in the Empire as a whole. The 5.3 million Germans were more than matched by 3.3 million Magyars and 2.5 million Czechs. The other nationalities tilted the balance even further away from the ruling Germans. The only time that Britain faced a situation remotely like this was between the Irish Union and the Famine, when a serious rivalry in population existed. In the Habsburg lands the lack of one clear dominant nationality became even further marked in the nineteenth century, when, in the aftermath of the disasterous defeat at the hands of Bismarck at Sadowa in 1866 the idea of a dual-monarchy, sharing power with the Magyars, had to be accepted. Austria- Hungary survived for over 50 years. England-Scotland or England-Ireland never really existed in the sense of a dual monarchy, except in the mind of Arthur Griffith who used Austria-Hungary as the inspiration of the original Sinn Fein. England-Wales is not even worth considering. The idea of a multinational kingdom is a good stick with which to beat the grosser manifestations of cultural chauvinism in England, but it is rather a blunt instrument for the comparative analysis of the British experience.

These comparative questions cannot be pursued further here. The concern in what follows in this introduction will be to set the other papers in a wider historical framework by reviewing the themes that have emerged from the literature on the nature of the British state. They do not exhaust the subject but they do lead us into its central issues. Three themes are given attention.

(1)   The integration of the United Kingdom.
(2)   Regional identities and the pattern of core-periphery relationships
(3)   The problem of England within the United Kingdom

The Integration of the United Kingdom

The United Kingdom is a centralised state. It should, however, be emphasised that centralisation does not imply total uniformity. Scotland has a different legal and educational system from England and Wales, and a different religion is established there from in England. In Wales, since 1920, there has been no religious establishment at all and in Ireland the religious establishment was destroyed half a century before the independence of the 26 counties was achieved. Wales, Scotland and Northern Ireland are administered largely through devolved government departments and for half a century (1921-1972), Northern Ireland had a devolved, elected, government. Further examples of this diversity could be given, but they would not influence the overall judgement of the successful achievement of centralisation- indeed the examles given tend to reinforce the legitimacy of central government rather than to challenge it. Keith Robbins has recently examined the competing forces of integration and diversity in nineteenth-century Britain and his conclusion that the outbreak of the First World War showed the strength of the integration is unexceptionable.

The process by which political integration was achieved has not been very fully explored. The oldest centripetal force is the monarchy. The Saxon kingdoms struggled for overall supremacy and in the process created a single entity within their territory. The Normans took over this structure, and the political struggles of the middle ages were almost invariably for the control of this state rather than for its break up. The Conquest destroyed the territorial basis of the aristocracy and with it their close identity with particular regions. The struggle became one for a say in the government of the kingdom, rather than for seperate forms of government. As Samuel Finer puts it neatly, on this side of the Channel there was a struggle for "voice" while in France the alternative of "exit" was more widely used. Provincial assemblies gained power there and it took the revolution of 1789 to dislodge them. In England and Wales the sole example of the "exit" option was the proposed Tripartite Indenture of 1403, when Owain Glyndwr, the Mortimers and the Percies envisaged a three way carve up of the kingdom. Even in this Mortimer would have retained a vestigal kingship at the centre.

Medieval communications and institutions of government did not allow the King's writ to run with the same force everywhere. The delegation of some of the royal powers to palatinates and marcher lords effectively gave the crown a wider reach, though with some transmission losses in the exercise of power. The King retained always his rights over treason, and the fact that marcher lords also held other lands in the royal domain gave a greater influence over them. The destruction of these liberties was largely the work of Thomas Cromwell and the Reformation Parliament. Two acts in 1536 saw the end of the marcher lords and the real power of the palatinates. In the next decade, the crown would claim Ireland as its own, and by then the dynastic alliance which would ultimately join the thrones of Scotland and England had already been made. Wales had acknowledged the overlordship of the English crown since the time of Alfred, and not even the Princes of Gwynedd in the 13th century had tried to overturn that, for all their concern to create a Welsh feudal state. The Tudor Revolution in government was a process of the concentration of power in the hands of the King in parliament. It was often brutal and despotic but it never succeeded in becoming a fully-fledged absolutism.

One of the first issues to confront this transformed Tudor state was the very one that had created it- religion. The Reformation was supported by some popular enthusiasm and a heritage of Lollardism, but this was not evenly spread, either geographically or socially. It tended to concentrate in the southern and eastern parts and amongst the trading classes though it was far from absent in the northern diocese of York. The north and the west rose in rebellion against royal supremacy and the new theology of the prayer book. Religious uniformity was imposed by harsh and sometimes treacherous repression. The lack of any rising in Wales and the influence of its humanist scholars over government led to the implantation of protestantism through the Welsh language, via a Welsh translation of the Bible and Prayer Book. Cromwell's centralising neatness was qualified by this Elizabethan settlement of religion. The breadth of that protestant settlement was an attempt to ensure a minimum integration over religious issues, but it was combined with a novel tendency to see Catholics as traitors. Adherence to the one state church became a test of orthodoxy in England and Wales until the legislation requiring attendance (and its later Restoration accretions) was formally repealed in 1828-9. In Wales uniformity had been tempered by the use of another language. Once Scotland entered the Kingdom, it was impossible to insist on religious uniformity there, given its later, more violent and theologically more intense Reformation. It was in Ireland that there were the strongest attempts to root out religious heterodoxy- its staunch Catholicism. The stategem of the selective planting of protestants in key areas was followed by the steady accumulation of land in protestant hands and the protestant ascendancy was formally imposed in legal codes fron 1691 to 1778. Yet Catholic religious observance was never effectively repressed.

The attempt to establish a coherent pattern of religion in these islands by Charles I and Archbishop Laud had contributed to the outbreak of the Civil War. Parallel attempts to centralise power and to break with what were seen as established traditions of consent in taxation, also had their part to play. The Civil War exposed the limits of centralisation, and the real power which remained in the periphery. It was, in the title of a John Morrill's book, *The Revolt of the Provinces*. In the outcome the King in Parliament remained the supreme power, but the balance shifted decisively to parliament. This assembly was an effective means of integrating those provinces through representatives of local and county communities. The price was the easing of executive control of those communities. Again the obverse of a tradition of centralisation was the toleration of a certain amount of diversity.

The Union with Scotland and the Jacobite rebellions of 1715 and 1745 posed the problem of the integration of the Highlands. Lowlanders joined or even initiated the assault on a society and its culture. Military roads, the banning of the tartan and the pipes, and the spread of English language education all had their role to play. By the early nineteenth century, some of these symbols were so devoid of meaning that they could be appropriated by the Edinburgh elite as symbols of Scotland's survival within the Hanoverian United Kingdom. George IV 's visit in 1822, the first by a Hanoverian king, established the tradition, and was commemorated in statuary. The movement of Englishmen northwards for education in the superior universities of the north, and the claims to Scots ancestry of many of the governors added to the process. Scottish intellectuals like Hume and Smith sent their ideas to England while later thinkers like Carlyle took the road south. North Britain reached its peak in the Victorian era, was sanctified by a royal seal of approval at Balmoral, and imitated by the grouse shooting and stag painting classes. In 1921, in the midst of the Irish crisis, Lloyd George found it easy to assemble a cabinet meeting in Scotland during the summer recess. Ultimately the trickle of tourists became a flood. Scotland's place in the country of the nineteenth century mind had become secure. Scott's novels, Burns' poems, Wilkie and Landseer's paintings, along with Mendelssohn's music ensured that this was the case.

Wales never made it to quite the same degree in terms of images. There was Thomas Pennant of course, and a whole host of following tour writers; there was 'poor Wilson' and his artistic followers, but music came only in the form of the male-voice choir, taking its trophies at Crystal Palace. In the literary sense Wales scarcely existed through the medium of English until the twentieth century. Wales won through into recognition in the political sphere and forced itself on the wider world after 1840. My paper explores some aspects of this process. Celts were accepted into the English family by Matthew Arnold, as long as they forsook their native language; their literature (in translation) and their aristocratic attitudes along with their anti-utilitarian stance were seen as vital aspects of the process of constructing a civilisation out of nineteenth century industrial society. Wales and Scotland could be accepted in their different ways, but Ireland proved more indigestible.

The basic reasons were Catholicism, the lack of industrialisation, and the geography of an island which encouraged the image of a seperate political entity. The first formed the basis of a spectacular and protracted political mobilisation, but one that aimed at a radical re-negotiation of the union, rather than a more comfortable place within it. The second gave Ireland economic interests different from the bulk of the British Isles; the scar of the Famine was not easily eradicated. The process of modernisation tended to reduce the gap between the constituent parts of the British Isles in the course of the century, but the European crisis of the 1910-20 provided the opportunity for a *putsch* which ultimately attracted broader support. A body blow seemed to have been dealt to the Union, but in the event, it survived. Indeed the motor for dramatic change in Wales and Scotland was removed once the Irish question seemed to have been consigned to the dustbin of history in 1922. The early experience of the Free State was hardly an inspiration either. The exception which proves the first two rules is of course the north-east of the island. The protestant and industrial forces which gathered here were sufficient to overwhelm the sense of identity of an island, and the longer that the border has existed, the more people's perceptions of Ireland have altered to accommodate this fact- except, of course, for Republicans. The ties that continue to bind Ulster (and the attitudes which distinguish it) are sensitively explored by Harvey Cox is his essay.

The place of Wales in the structure of the United Kingdom in the past hundred years is Emyr Williams's concern. As against a dominant view which has bemoaned the waning of Welsh national consciousness in the 20th century with the weakening of religion and the Welsh language, he sees certain positive features in the current situation- the emergence of a battery of institutions, and the opportunity to make positive use of them if they can be subjected to democratic control. John Osmond in his essay echoes some of these points in a more detailed look at the current situation. Yet these Welsh state institutions are relatively new and they occur in a context which includes powerful articulators of a British identity- the B.B.C., for instance. However it seems evident that the period of maximum effectiveness of such stimuli has passed. Colin McCabe has located the era of the final flowering of the B.B.C.'s evocation of national unity in the early days of the T.V. duopoly. Since then a fragmentation of publics has occured. One consequence of this is the space which S4C now occupies. Cable and satellite T.V. throw up many alternative possibilities, the results of which are hard to predict, but they do not presage a return to a Reithian British consensus.

Core-Periphery and the Question of Regional Identity

In the most general terms, there is no disputing where the core of the British/ English state is located. Its origins in the south-eastern portion of the the larger island have never been transcended. The exact delimitation is more contentious. Michael Hechter's identification of the core with England is clearly inadequate and has been generally rejected as being too wide in its geographical reach. On the other hand the definition preferred by Jim Bulpitt and Richard Rose which puts it firmly in the square mile or so around Westminster and gives it a parliamentary and Whitehall axis, is far too narrow. It leaves out of account any notion of the control of this state by a particular class or the territory that it dominates. It is possible to refer to an economic core and a political core, as does Christopher Smout, but in most periods of British history they shared the same general location. The south-eastern corner of the island attracted invaders and the Thames Valley gave access to the interior. It formed the base for any wider conquest, and its rulers benefitted from the resources at their backs. Alfred's rearguard action against the Danes fell back thus far and no further. From London and Winchester the reconquest was orchestrated. The grip of the medieval kings was firmest on the territory closest to this area, and they used a variety of expedients to hold on to the further reaches of England. They sometimes ventured north to show their presence and to consume the feudal obligations they were owed *in situ*, but the monarchy remained rooted in the south-eastern corner. It may have been an exaggeration for observers to say that the north knew no king save a Percy and a Neville, but it was not a complete distortion.

For most people, of course, the social world was more limited than that of the realm. Alan Everitt has shown that we need to think of the *pays*; and when 16th and 17th century men and women referred to their country, it was the agricultural region of the *pays* that they meant. At most it was the county. Counties were made up of *pays*; often focussed on a major market town which marked the junction of two major areas with different products which could be traded. Regions were the products of industrialisation which crossed the old boundaries of *pays* and county. Often coalfields gave them unity. Canal systems connected them to the

13

sea without the need to go through London. The rise of a conglomeration of such regions in the north of England and the Celtic areas in the century after 1780 allowed the major challenge to the dominance of the south-east that there has ever been in the history of Britain to be mounted.

The Victorian saying, 'What Manchester says today, the rest of the world says tomorrow' was as an indication of the power shift. There were aspirations from the more visionary Victorian enthusiasts that Manchester and Liverpool could merge and become a new capital. The combined weight of Liverpool, Manchester, Leeds, Bradford, Sheffield and Hull seemed to tilt the scales. Cardiff, Belfast and especially Glasgow made them drop decisively. The north-south divide of the present era- so much to the advantage of the south now, the reverse of the nineteenth century image- has made historians more tentative or even to wonder whether anything fundamental really changed in the last century. Keith Robbins feels that, like the poor in general, the north-south divide has always been with us. Francis Sheppard has emphasised the extent to which real power still resided in London in the 19th century. Bill Rubinstein has stressed the fact that the largest fortunes were made in the City and not in northern industry. C.H. Lee has even found the south's economic structure, with its dominance by the service sector, to be a harbinger of the future prosperity; it is a far cry from the old emphasis on the poverty of the nineteenth century south, whether in the grain-growing regions or in the casual labour market of London. Southall has stressed the extent of unemployment in the Victorian and Edwardian north, finding in it a prefiguration of the thirties' crisis. Some of it also seems to be anachronistic, an attempt to explain away industrial decline and the dominance of the north by a pretence that it never happened in the first place, but that cannot be pursued here. Whatever the situation in the first three quarters of the last century (and they need a great deal of further exploration), trends since then have restored the south to its ancient dominance. By the depression of the interwar years, this was abundantly clear; the migrants from the depressed areas, and the hunger marchers, both acknowledged the fact. Now the gap between the south-east and the rest of the kingdom is widening, and that is more significant than the divide between the nations of Wales, Scotland, Northern Ireland and England in economic terms. All this is tending to make mobilisation on the basis of territory more significant than it has been in the recent past. Not only Scotland and Wales are demanding representative assemblies, but so is a group in the North, and they have secured the support of some of the region's M.P.s. Industrial decline has muted some of the class antagonisms of industry, and it is not an infrequent thing to find the regional T.U.C. allied with its C.B.I. counterpart to influence government. In Scotland the long-established national T.U.C. has proved to be effective in mobilising a wider coalition of forces on many occasions.

English Identity and Nationalism

The Norman Conquest greatly complicated the problems of English identity. The old Saxon state (along with its Danish intrusions) was conquered by a people whose political aspirations spanned the English Channel. They did not lose these territories in France until 1204 and their Plantagenet successors continued to pursue aims in France in the 14th and 15th centuries. The French connection did not finally cease until the Pale of Calais was lost under Mary Tudor in the 1550s. The identity of the monarchy and its subjects with a particular territory was therefore something which was not easy to achieve. Conventionally England eventually became identified as an island (despite being only part of one in fact) but this was not easily done. The island situation was still seen as a weakness for much of the middle ages. After all it was the long sea coast that had attracted the successive waves of invaders, and observers had been inclined to see the coast as making the inhabitants rather visionary- one almost said wet- rather than sturdy sea-dogs. The conquest also imposed a radical duality of language on the territory and this was not overcome until English began to surface in the 14th century, but its evolution into a recognisably modern form was not completed until Renaissance conceptions of grammar were imposed upon it in the 16th century. Chaucer had wondered whether the people of the north would understand his verse; most scholars seem to doubt it. Any notion of standard English was a later development, and as Raymond Williams has shown, the product of a bourgeois quest for respectabliity in the period since the 18th century.

English identity did not, therefore, arise easily and ready made; its creation was essentially the work of the later middle ages and the 16th century. By the 15th century overseas observers were beginning to find touches of that typical feeling of superiority over foreigners and a desire to export English models of government. The long-term result of continental defeat was to turn attention towards the island for which the sea now provided a welcome bastion. The defeat of the Armada in 1588 ultimately consolidated that myth. Once attention had focussed on the island a fairly coherent idea of identity could evolve. There had been no great physical barriers to be overcome within England, and the state became the most centralised in Europe. The limit was the amount of territory which the institutions of rule could realistically control. The geographical periphery of England was placed under the control of agents to whom royal authority was delegated- marcher lords, and the lay and clerical rulers of the Counties Palatinate. Protestantism, another key ingredient of the mix of identity, was a product of the same era. Perhaps only the Irish fully understand what a key aspect of Englishness it actually is. Deliverance from Spain and the Counter-Reformation encouraged the idea that there was a divinely appointed English mission against Rome. By the end of the century Shakespeare could write much of the mythology of the ruling dynasty and their territory, most famously his evocation of the 'sceptr'd isle', one of the most enduring symbols of English identity. He also condemned the political mayhem that had characterised England in the past, to the benefit of the Tudors' subsequent polished performance.

Yet English identity, had from the beginning, to share its space with an alternative conception- the older Celtic notion of Britishness. In the major lull in England's involvement with France in the middle ages there had been an increase in conflict with the Celtic periphery. The native rulers of Wales had been subjugated by the increased power of the Crusading military machine, which could draw resources from the international capital of its day, the bankers of the northern Italian cities. Scotland nearly suffered a similar fate but its superior political organisation and the difficulties which its geography presented to lasting conquest probably saved it. Edward I sharpened a sense of English identity in hammering the Scots and the Welsh. It was a conscious rallying cry; not for nothing do the National Front celebrate him as a

'Great English Racist'.

Yet there were also borrowings from these territories. The conception of an island occupied by an ancient British race with glories in its past was a seductive one. In the 12th century Geoffrey of Monmouth had put the legends into written form and they served many uses. In the frequent eras of internal disorder in the middle ages the Arthurian legend was adopted as a binding and legitimating force. The key moments were the 'anarchy' of Stephen and Matilda's civil wars of the 12th century, and the Wars of the Roses.

By the time of the Reformation there were even more uses. What better justification was there for the break with Rome than that of ancient British traditions of independence? Reformation statutes gave the mythology of Geoffrey a life not only beyond the grave, but beyond the destructive research of Polydore Virgil, the Renaissance historian who had already exploded Geoffrey's imaginative approach to the past. The ancient Welsh myth of the discovery of America by Madoc ap Llywelyn in 1170 served a similar purpose in the Tudor era of emerging imperial rivalries. The accession of a nominally Welsh dynasty in 1485 and of a genuinely Scottish one in 1603 only compounded the problem of a distinctly English identity. The latter revived the idea of Great Britain in a formal sense.

Yet an English myth had already appeared and the bitter conflicts of the 17th century were to put it at the heart of political discussion. The claims of Parliament in the English Revolution rested essentially on the idea of an ancient constitution enshrined in Magna Carta and the Petition of Right as well as more generally in the common law. Radicals went beyond this to claim political rights for 'freeborn Englishmen'. This myth rested on a distinctly English conception of history taking its cue from the Saxon Witan, and suspicious of the later invaders- tyrants who had imposed the 'Norman Yoke' upon them. The mission of the English was to restore these lost rights. After the Second Civil War it was essentially these rival conceptions of Englishness that were at stake. Here were some clear senses of being English, which carried political implications and at least an embryonic nationalism. The older views of Britishness were tainted by their association with the absolutism of the Tudors. Yet notions of Englishness still had to operate in a wider context. The English Revolution was conceivable only in the context of the 'War of the Three Kingdoms': without Scottish invasion and Irish rebellion it could not have happened. The whole conflict was to a large extent provoked by the problems of a multiple kingdom in which the monarchy could not reconcile the claims of three competing religions.

The long-term consequences of this revolution magnified this conflict of identities between England and Britain. Firstly, it led to the creation of an Empire which always seems to have been regarded as British rather than English. Secondly, Scotland and England were united in 1707. The economic crisis of the turn of the 18th century had hit Scotland hard, and in reality its fortunes were now tied closely to those of England. The need to avert the possibility of a Jacobite succession to the throne of Scotland when Queen Anne died gave the idea some impetus south of the border too; the terms were to be largely those of England rather than the federal union that many Scots politicians had wanted. In the end it was Hobson's choice. The consequence of this was a new effloresence of the idea of Britishness. Scots sought to win a place in England (and in the sun) by assimilating both counties to a common past. They were not Scots but a variant of the same stock- North Britons. Jointly they were symbolised by Britannia who ruled the waves. This effort came largely from north of the border, for in England this was the century of that distinctively English figure of John Bull. He was distinguised from foreigners by his roast beef and leather shoes but from Scots by his familiarity with privvies and other forms of civilisation. In the 1760s the Wilkite movement used such English sentiments as a means to rally opposition to George III and his Scottish Prime Minister, Lord Bute. When Wilkes called his anti-government periodical *The North Briton*, it was not with the intent of assimilation. However, by the 1790s, English radicals would use the term 'British' positively in order to garner support in Scotland.

Most of this discussion has concerned national identities rather than of nationalism. Hans Kohn in his classic article on the growth of English nationalism argued that it had become fully fledged in the revolution of the 17th century and had united the whole people. His evidence for this is rather sketchy and it depends heavily on the massive buttress of John Milton. He pays no regard to the overlapping British identity, and of course popular nationalism on the principles of 1776 and 1789 failed to break through in England. The Levellers, who advocated something like this, were defeated by Cromwell's military power. The evidence for the survival of their legacy is sketchy. The creed of popular sovreignty, the cornerstone of one kind of nationalism, was the product of the late 18th century upheavals and arguably this never washed up on these shores- or at least it was repulsed with the French landings of 1797-8. Tom Paine, one of the creators of the idea, had a massive impact in the 1790s but he never displaced entirely the numerous variations on the theme of the freeborn Englishman. Paine's direct successors were sectarians like Carlile, more intent on purity than populism. The popular mantle went to 'the Great Cobbett' who never shook himself free of a certain John Bullishness and who looked resolutely back to a past happier society. He venerated Paine, and the people against 'the thing' but in an important sense lost Paine's real rationalist and constitutionalist legacy as well as his bones. Chartism was perhaps the last real chance for a popular creed to break through; it divided Britain into a popular majority and a narrow group of rulers rather than into economic classes. After its demise economic conflict came to dominate the approach of the labour movement. It tended to take the institutions of the state for granted and to assume that they could become instruments for the enactment of socialism. Actually they were increasingly serving other purposes.

The failure to develop any lasting popular nationalism , or the base of a written constitution, left a vacuum in British political life. The rulers were reluctant, initially, to fill it with state-sponsored effusions of loyalty for they still feared patriotism as a popular force. This is what the Tory Dr. Johnson was also refering to in his frequently misunderstood declaration during the Falklands crisis of 1770 that 'patriotism was the last refuge of the scoundrel'. Wilkes was a patriot, and so were the leaders of the French Revolution of 1789. Country was venerated above the interests of the current rulers, and indeed used as a weapon against them. The first hesitating steps away from this were seen in the later stages of the reign of George III. The King was an unusual one for the time. Firstly he had been born in Britain, an almost unique distinction in the 18th century. Secondly his madness made him politically impotent and he therefore acquired a symbolic quality of being above the party squabble. Its onset in 1788-9 was fortuitously timed for him to become the father of his people against the paricidal French. The third element of distinctivness, the probity of his family life enabled him to play the paternal role. The management of this role was largely a matter of private enterprise- the erection of memorials to the 50th anniversary of his succession and other ceremonials. Whatever he achieved in this sphere, however, the Prince Regent automatically dissipated. George's apotheosis pointed to the future role of the monarchy, but it would not be until 100 years after the first onset of his madness that the harvest would be gathered. In between, the fortunes of the monarchy fell to a low ebb. Its ceremonial was incompetent to an incredible degree, and Victoria's widowly seclusion undid any good that Albert's modernising attitudes might have done. Victoria's Golden Jubilee in 1887 was viewed as a political gamble- would she be booed on the streets?- but turned into a triumph. It provided reassurance in a world where Britain's economic lead was already being reduced. Ceremonial became increasingly rehearsed and slick. New media carried it far and wide thereafter. Victoria's funeral in 1901 was a chance for moving pictures. Radio developed hushed royal tones from the beginning. Television turned the Coronation of 1953 into a triumphant celebration of the end of austerity.

Monarchy, therefore, came to symbolise the nation. It took the place of the people. They became a stage army for jingoism - 'Soldiers of the Queen'. There was always an imperial resonance to this and it became inextricably mixed with ideas of racial superiority. Again Englishness had become merged in a wider identity- the Empire and the white race. There were also wider cultural underpinnings. Folklore collectors, literary critics, composers, historians and guide book writers created a strong cultural sense of England and its distinctiveness. Much of it was appropriated for imperial concerns, as with the celebration of representative institutions in Stubbs's version of English history, and the more triumphant pieces of Elgar. Yet the popular potential in this for political mobilisation remained limited. The confusion of England and Britain was endless and often irritating to the English. When Stanley Baldwin addressed the Royal Society of St. George at the Hotel Cecil in 1924 he rejoiced that he was free to use the term 'England' and not constrained to speak of 'Britain'. This is a very clear example of the suppressed nationalism that Bernard Crick discusses below.

The notion of a popular creed of the English nation never completely died, however. We can see it distinctly in William Morris's socialist ideas and in the very title of Blatchford's 'Merrie England'. Its flowering was in World War Two. Michael Foot and others' quest for "Guilty Men" had conscious echoes of the popular citizenship of the French Revolution about it. The army was the most radical and argumentative since the 1640s. A vital part of the myth of Dunkirk was that the people in their little boats had done what the mighty and powerful had failed to do. Film makers of the phoney war period frequently picked out the upper classes as the potential fifth columnists; only the people could be trusted. J.B. Priestley's powerful and widely listened to radio broadcasts distinguised clearly between the people and the classes in a manner that might have moved the Chartists. Virtue clearly lay with the people. Orwell explored sensitively the idea of the English nation in his fine pamphlet *The Lion and the Unicorn*; his vision of radical democracy was enshrined in the ideal of a citizen with the rifle behind the door. Similar concerns had influenced the creation of the Home Guard (though perhaps the very title, lacking any real connection with the French and American National Guards is also significant). At the end of this 'people's war', the N.C.B. came to manage the mines on behalf of the people. The failure of those enterprises to win a wider popular base is indicative of a general failing in Britain, the inability to create a lasting and popular nationalism. England is a powerful idea, with no decent means to mobilisation. Even the National Front tends to stress Britain. So does the Prime Minister. 'Brit'n' is so often on her lips that we are sometimes unsure about whether she is invoking the spirit of the nation, or summoning her new European Commissioner. Ready obedience is expected from both; neither Britain nor England currently seem to have the potential for genuine popular mobilisation.

Conclusion

The United Kingdom, therefore, exhibits a strong degree of integration, though it achieves this partly by means of tolerating diversity. It has, for most (if not all) of its existence been dominated economically by the south-eastern portion of England. This has frequently produced tensions within the polity, and in the 19th and early 20th centuries it proved impossible to reconcile most of Ireland to membership of that polity. In this diverse structure the idea of England is ever-present, but is rarely asserted positively because of the problem of reconciling the other peoples to its numerical, economic and cultural dominance. This makes the expression of regional interests most difficult in the north of England because of the lack of an appropriate cultural lever such as the Celtic countries have often used to their advantage. There are some periods when the United Kingdom reconciles its diversity better than at others. We are currently in a period of conflict and tension.

What the future holds for the British state is not easy to say. The oscillations of opinion in the past decade are a warning against glib answers. The emphasis on 'the break-up of Britain', so fashionable in the 70s was replaced by Rose and Bulpitt's academic statement of the Unionism in the early 80s. In that context- Thatcherite centralisation and the defeat of the devolution movements- these arguments seemed to carry all before them. Since then the political visibility of north-south divide (exacerbated by the free market) the wider interest raised by the political situation in Scotland, along with the stagnation and frustration of conventional Labour politics has put the centripetal case back on the agenda. The peripheral perspective of the decentralisers of the 70s has now been replaced by a wider concern to understand the whole union and its consequences. The centre has come under much closer scrutiny too. Out of this should come a firmer understanding of the diversity of the identities in these islands, the ties that bind them together, and the tensions that force them apart. These papers make a contribution to that process of understanding the immediate past and the present. Whichever direction we may decide to go in the future, we will be better prepared for the journey by knowing something of from where we set out.

AN ENGLISHMAN CONSIDERS HIS PASSPORT

BERNARD CRICK

You and I, whatever our politics, are legal citizens of a state with no agreed colloquial name. Our passports call us citizens of "The United Kingdom of Great Britain and Ireland". But what does one reply when faced by that common existential question of civilized life, which is neither precisely legal nor precisely philosophical, found in foreign hotel registers, "Nationality?"

If that question is meant to establish legal citizenship, then "British" is correct, although that is the least used name colloquially for people as distinct from goods, except in the expletive form of "Brits" which now used not merely by Aussies but by both Prods and Taigs in Ulster. But many write in the register not "British", but "Scottish" or "Welsh" The question does, after all, ask "Nationality?" And when those with an address in Northern Ireland write "British" one reasonably assumes that they are Protestant and Unionist. And a few with similar addresses boldly write "Irish", and some of those even carry, quite legally, an Irish passport instead of or even as well as a United Kingdom passport. Once or twice I've seen entries which slide around the question and write "citizen of the United Kingdom", which means that they are either a Catholic who is an Alliance Party supporter or that even rarer stubborn breed, a Scottish Tory. Once I read "Cornish" but I suspected, correctly, that it was a wag and not a nut.

The majority write "English". The overwhelming majority of United Kingdom passport holders are, of course, "English"; but I have a suspicion that many of them write "English" not as an assertion of nationality, as do those who write Irish, Scottish or Welsh, but out of a common but mistaken belief that "English" is the noun or adjective corresponding to "citizen of the United Kingdom of Great Britain and Northern Ireland". This angers me personally: my children are half Welsh, I live in Edinburgh from choice and visit Ireland frequently, often for pleasure. And it angers me intellectually: I believe that the United Kingdom is a multi-national state or a union of different nations with different cultures

23

and different histories. For I like it that way - even though I note that school books in History and Politics south of the border (sorry, I mean that border just north of the Roman wall) are almost entirely Anglocentric.

Leave aside, for the moment, whether this union was a free and voluntary contract in a manner that would have satisfied the philosophical criteria of John Locke (plainly not). When I retired from London University to live in Scotland my colleagues gave me a Gillray cartoon called "The Union Club" which shows satirically the living and the dead notables of English and Irish politics drinking wildly together, Pitt and Grattan hand in hand, rival bishops sharing pipes, a busty Brittania and a buxom Hibernia amorously lip to lip, Lord Edward and Wolfe Tone jigging towards a sodden Prince and a collapsed Fox, as if the Union was a cause for mutual congratulation (as the Act or Treaty of Union with Scotland of 1707 had been - well, on the whole: most Scots at the time, real history now tells us, thought that they had driven a sensible bargain). And even leave aside, for a moment too, the special problem of Northern Ireland. If the Irish remember their history too obsessively, ordinary English people forget theirs too easily; but when English politicians forget (as they have done in the last decade) that they are dealing with a union of peoples and not (whatever the state myths) an homogenous society with a centralised and common administration (Scotland, Wales and Northern Ireland - not to mention, as politically trivial but extraordinary, the Channel Islands and the Isle of Man!), trouble can follow. Thatcherism represents a conservatism that has forgotten true history and is living its myths. She believes that formal sovereignty is not merely inalienable (shades of "The Treaty"!) but is the same as effective political power, and that the liberating of market forces has removed any vestigial need for the political articulation of different cultures.

Even in documents more elaborate than a passport we English are very confused when we try to name our state. The Central Office of Information publishes an annual handbook on the United Kingdom which has all kinds of useful information in it, and has a wide circulation abroad. The title of it is bizarrely (though no one notices or complains) the name of a former Roman province, which has no modern legal or

24

precise geographical meaning, *Britain*. The current preface of *Britain* states:

> Care should be taken when studying British statistics to note whether they refer to England, to England and Wales ...., to Great Britain, which comprises England, Wales and Scotland, or to the United Kingdom (which is the same as Britain, that is Great Britain and Northern Ireland) as a whole.

Indeed. But is "Britain" usually used as "The same as" the United Kingdom as a whole? When I say "Britain" I mean, contrary to the C.O.I., the mainland only and say "Great Britain" when I want to include Northern Ireland. Perhaps usage varies. In the *Oxford English Dictionary* early usages of Britain all refer to the island or the mainland of the archipelago. And *O.E.D.*'s summary of early modern usage is confused: "The proper name of the whole island, containing England, Wales and Scotland, with their dependencies; more fully called Great Britain; now used for the British state or Empire as a whole." That "more fully" is as a dictionary entry politically very question-begging and pre-emptive. "Britain" and "Great Britain" are as often used to refer to different entities. Ulster Loyalists are always careful to proclaim their (conditional) loyalty to "Great Britain" or "The United Kingdom"; they rightly suspect that loose talk of "Britain" can often mean the mainland alone, and thus prove a device to distance them, ultimately to separate them.

The fundamental problem is not, of course, even as simple as that of maintaining or recovering a true view of Great Britain as a multi-national society and, in many respects, a quasi-federal polity. For it is also a problem of the interrelations of "these islands" or, since usage creates names more than justice, the British Isles. For this brief argument it is necessary to say no more than that the cultural and social relations of the Republic of Ireland and Great Britain have been and are likely to remain (whatever ultimately happens to or in Northern Ireland) relations of an intimacy unusual, though not entirely unprecedented, between different legally sovereign states. If the *Gaeltacht* had ever become all Ireland as the heroes of 1916 (forgetting Connolly) believed, the situation would be different; but it didn't. And it would be different again, more difficult even, if standard English language and literature

25

had not been profoundly influenced by the vigour of Irish, Scottish and Welsh English. There is much talk always in British political circles of "the special relationship" with the United States. But this concept is as true of Britain and Ireland together. And, moreover, the special Irish relationship with the United States and the special British relationship to the United States coexist and condition each other; to see them only as rivals is simplistic, culturally and politically mistaken. Most American opinion values both and resents the jealous quarrels of its two most honoured elderly and difficult relatives.

An often forgotten part of the problem of the interrelations of the nations of the British Isles is a lack of clarity by the English of what constitutes their own national identity. They could perhaps deal more easily and justly with the others if they were more clear about their own nature. And, by the way, relationships are reciprocal: a knowledge of England and the English is necessary to deal with the English, even where knowledge is wholly unclouded by affection. Was it Orwell who said to Koestler or Koestler to Orwell, "know thy enemy as thyself". Welsh Nationalists have a great advantage in this respect over both Nationalist and Unionist politicians in Ulster. Somehow it is further, in terms of social distance, from Belfast to London than it is from Bangor or Harlech, despite the language question. And Dublin, in some ways, is closer than either. Perhaps people who are securely a different world can understand others better than those who describe their own identity mainly by negative exclusions: "No Pope" or "Brits Out". Welsh-speaking Welsh and Irish in the Republic may understand the English better than most English do themselves. They have had to and have had a lot of experience. The English enjoy the others when in holiday mood.

In all this one must distinguish, however, between feelings of national identify and "nationalism". By "nationalism" I mean, no more or no less, than the doctrine that for every nation there must be a state. For about three hundred years the mainland United Kingdom, at least, and including those in Northern Ireland who want to be included in it, has shown that while the nationalist theory of the state is a common aspiration, it is not a universal rule. And there are many other contrary examples: Belgium and Canada, for instance. (And there would seem no possible peaceful way forward for South Africa and for Israel/Palestine except as multi-national states; both are areas, like Northern Ireland, where claims to sovereignty are part of the problem, not the solution). That question in the foreign hotel register does make a nationalist assumption that nation and legal citizenship should normally go together and be exclusive: that is why the different entries are emblematic of the difficulties in these islands, so long, that is, as one is only allowed one answer.

Most English left-wing authors used to regard any discussion their own national identity as subversive of the purity of the Word and a distraction from the Good News of the class struggle. I am nearly sixty. All my adult life I have found that most of my fellow English left-wing intellectuals are suckers for anybody else's nationalism and contemptuous of (and what is sometimes even more dangerous, ignorant of) their own. Only recently have a few emerged who are not positively embarrassed by patriotism. As a political philosopher I use the word "sucker" quite technically; I mean that they ingest other people's nationalisms whole as a conditioned reflex. Instead of being critical friends of liberation movements, occasionally asking whether one party states always make the best decisions, whether autocracy is always efficient, whether bombs are always the best persuaders and terror always the best answer to terror, they tend almost to revel in justifying other people's violence. David Caute once defined the Fellow Travellers of the 1930s as those who believed in socialism in somebody else's country.

If the left were always true heirs of the Enlightenment and of the Declaration of the Rights of Man, as at their best they are, they would say that any nationalism has to be pursued by means compatible with liberty, justice and respect for the rights of others - whether individuals or groups, especially groups who embarrassingly regard themselves as nations but happen to share the same sacred soil. And the English left-wing enjoy being made to feel guilty for the sins of their colonialist fathers. It is almost too easy to make us feel guilty. Some Irish writers are expert in this - and some Scots and Welsh too, only fewer people listen. But guilt for sins one has not committed oneself is an insecure basis (I am not Christian enough to believe otherwise) for what has to be a close relationship. Indeed guilt even for one's own sins it is rarely a healthy basis for a continuing relationship of any kind (I am Christian enough to believe that repentance, forgiveness and mercy are necessary virtues, even in political life).

The only English left-wing writer to defend English patriotism and to try to characterise its legitimate content, sardonically, sensitively and, on the whole, sensibly, was George Orwell in his *The Lion and the Unicorn*. A few English right-wing authors have celebrated England specifically, notably Arthur Bryant and A.L. Rowse and praised "the English national character" with the shameless reverence characteristic of nationalist literature. Their fitting reward was large sales of largely unread books purchased for, if not specifically produced for, private school prize givings. Yet there are very few serious studies of English character, still less of English dilemmas about identity. Considering that the English are not lacking in self esteem and, what A.L. Lowell once called, "a certain effortless sense of superiority", this is strange - but true. If you doubt this, try to compile a bibliography or look at any subject catalogue in a great library: sub-headings will show shelf-loads of books on Irish, Scottish and Welsh nationalism or national identity, not to mention French, German and American, etc. etc.; but very few, and then mostly rubbishy, on England and Englishness.

Why this massive silence? Why did the bulldog not bark even in the good old days when it could really bite? The explanation could lie in a very obvious factor. It is the simple presuppositions that we usually miss. Consider what historically, since at least the accession of James I and James VI to the two thrones, has been the main preoccupation of English politics: holding the United Kingdom together. Scotland and Ireland posed great problems for England even in the eighteenth and nineteenth centuries. And they both provoked alternating spasms of coercion and conciliation, occasionally both together. The former is better remembered than the latter, for obvious grim reasons. But if we compare British behaviour or policy with some other empires, then the degree of conciliation and the extent of devolved administration according to local customs, is equally remarkable. "Indirect Rule" can be derogated as "divide and rule" and dismissed as a mere tactic of colonialism. Whether the relationship of the English to the others is properly called colonial, whether it was that form of oppression, is a more difficult question than many admit. But most would admit that at least there is colonialism and colonialism. And that divide and rule usually meant the recognition and a minimal respect for pre-existing divisions, not their actual creation. Most reformers would rather see divisions swept away. But even if it was colonialist in spirit, the specific tactics pursued, the conciliation as well as the coercion, had lasting consequences, and to pursue it at all, whether in Ireland, Scotland, Wales or India imposed certain limitations on power.

For the English to have developed a strident literature of English nationalism, such as arose, often under official patronage, everywhere else in Europe, and in Ireland and Scotland, eventually in Wales, would have been divisive. From political necessity English politicians tried to develop a United Kingdom nationalism and, at least explicitly and officially, to identity themselves with it, wholeheartedly. But from the experience of dealing with Scotland in the seventeenth century and at least with the Old English and the new English in Ireland, the political tactic pursued was not that of colonial assimilation, but of a kind of cultural politics. Scots, Welsh and some Irish (all Irish after Catholic emancipation) were encouraged to have a dual sense of national identity. Tocqueville in his great *Democracy in America* saw this clearly in the contrast between French and British eighteenth century administration in North America.

When King James VI of Scotland had been proclaimed King of England it was not, as often said, as James I of England but as "James I, King of Great Britain". And that same formula was used throughout the Act or Treaty of Union in 1707, almost a pretence that "England" as a separate entity had gone out of business, whereas in 1603 a separate kingdom of Scotland was plainly acknowledged and in 1707 a formidable list of specifically Scottish rights were set down, including the establishment of the Presbyterian Church (which many Scots at the time saw as the real national institution, popular and representative, indeed, rather than the aristocratically dominated and corrupt Parliament). Throughout the eighteenth century English governments and courts, especially after the great scare of 1745, made conscious and strenuous efforts to establish "British" as the general description, and to replace "Scottish" and "English" with "North British" and "South British". Some Ministerial hacks even tried "West British" for Irish, or at least for Loyal Irish. But this early attempt at Newspeak collapsed by its own unreality hastened by waves of satire and ridicule. Only a hotel in Edinburgh survives to mark this usage, and the memory of John Wilkes's satiric and Scots-baiting *North Briton*. Policy soon swung the other way: to take pleasure in cultural diversity, the time of Ossian and the political patronage of romantic poets inventing past glories for the Celtic peoples.

Perhaps the high points of this cultural politics was when, after the repression of Highland Society, a cabinet decision was made to attempt toleration and reconciliation throughout Scotland. Sir Walter Scott, a firm but not uncritical Unionist, was given a commission by the cabinet to arrange and manage an official revival (sometimes invention) of traditional Scottish institutions, all to be ready for the visit of the appalling "Prinny", now George IV, to Edinburgh where he wore the kilt once - to the ribald delight of all cartoonists in the greatest age of English caricature. A pattern was set for the management of Irish and later Welsh affairs. This is well known. Enough to say that it went beyond folk songs in London drawing rooms and the wearing of the green by wives and daughters of some Viceroys. National cultural institutions were encouraged, up to a point.

If one looks for the missing dimension in all this, discussions of the English National character in the nineteenth century, then one must turn to the English novel. Novelists were much concerned with the character of the nations as well as of the classes, and the psychology of cross-pressured individuals. There was in England no state cult of nationalism with its sponsorship of official history and self-justificatory philosophy as found in France and Germany, and envied by subject peoples. (Only Coleridge did his private and eccentric best to fill the gap). To say however, that this lack of theoretical concern and philosophical explicitness was a product of English Toryism may be to reverse cause and effect. For royalists and absolutists in the seventeenth century had spilt as much ink and invoked at astonishing length quite as much scriptural authority and bad theology as did Parliament and Covenant men. If the main task of English Toryism was to keep the two, indeed the three, kingdoms together, a certain lack of theory was necessary, especially if theory could growingly take a cultural and national form.

30

Burke was to skate brilliantly to scratch over and cross-hatch some very opaque thin ice. He defended the rights of Irishmen, as he had the rights of the American colonists; but only within the framework of parliamentary sovereignty. English Tories, indeed the old Whigs too, basically held to two propositions: loyalty and sovereignty. Anything else was negotiable. Prudence and interest, said Burke, argued that sovereignty should not always be exercised; but its residual existence was essential and it could not be divided. He saw clearly that the whole doctrine of "Parliamentary sovereignty" had arisen as part of the 1688 Settlement of the "glorious because bloodless revolution" (bloodless in England, that is). Power could be delegated; federations were impossible in principle; but all power must be used with a restraint flowing from respect for and knowledge of traditional liberties, local customs and beliefs. Magnanimity in politics is not seldom the truest virtue, and "great empires and little minds go ill together." "I care not if you have a right to make them miserable; have you not an interest to make them happy?". "The use of force alone is but temporary. It may subdue for a moment, but it does not remove the necessity of subduing again: and a nation is not governed, which is perpetually to be conquered."

This fudge and toleration were part of English high politics. As the mediating institution the Tories looked somewhat more to the Crown (and themselves)) and the Whigs somewhat more to Parliament (and themselves). But neither wished to thrust a comprehensive English ideology on the other nations, so long as sovereign power was not challenged. The Irish Catholics posed a special difficulty to the English ruling class not because of their religion (the English rulers were not, after all, Presbyterians) but because of their international connections. So long as the Papacy even attempted, however spasmodically and ineffectually, to be an international political force, emancipation was not thought possible. Only after the Napoleonic Wars and the Congress of Vienna, when Great Britain emerged as an ally of "Legitimacy" against revolution principles, could she cease to fear continental intervention in Ireland.

What lay behind the cult of sovereignty as it was developed after 1688 by jurists and statesmen was something very deep in the English conservative mind. It was not the fear of any alternative social order but the fear of anarchy, of the sheer breakdown of authority. And the form it then took was not revolution, of course but a fear of the breakdown of the new United Kingdom: successful Scottish or Irish rebellion. Logically this is an odd argument. Why should the breakdown of the United Kingdom into separate states and distinct peoples and areas necessarily effect politically stability in England, or the trade, commerce and intercourse of its peoples? But in the circumstances of the eighteenth century international politics and war were inseparable from these questions. They are still sometimes confused, if with less plausibility. The historian Paul Kennedy's recent *The Rise and Fall of the Great Powers* became a best-seller probably because he sent a shiver of fear down the spines of affluent Americans: since all previous empires became economically overstretched and so declined, must not American hegemony go that way too? But Kennedy never says that the decline of an Empire necessarily leads to instability in the homeland and to barbarians coming over the wall. He is naughtily less than cautious, however, is not avoiding that sensational impression. But Great Britain is, after all, a clear enough example to the contrary.

If the English, however, for good reasons never developed a literature of English nationalism, they did develop a formidable substitute: in the late nineteenth century a literature of imperialism emerged which enjoyed considerable state patronage. Each of the nations of these islands could share in the imperial myth and reality. Most of Kipling's imperial stories contained a type from each of the nations: an English officer, a little slow and rigid but decent; a Scottish engineer, dour but resourceful; a Welsh N.C.O., cunning but dependable; and an Irish squaddie, coarse, comic but courageous. The English, make no mistake what I am saying, imposed their centralised politics on the other nations and the culture of their elite was on offer through the new Public Schools to the leaders of the other nations.

The English cult of the gentleman made its converts to a more political purpose in Scotland and Ireland than in France and Germany. But the old aristocratic ruling class tolerated, indeed often actively patronised and encouraged, Scottish, Welsh and Irish culture- so long as it did not threaten the unity of the state. And this was not purely instrumental. Tory district magistrates, whether in India or in Ireland, commonly studied and defended indigenous customs against the rationalising tendencies of liberal, Benthamite administrators, or sometimes against the Protestant missionaries and school masters. Perhaps the old Tories were so secure in themselves that they could often live, for a while (as in India before the Mutiny and the coming of the *Memsahibs* in two worlds, much as until the middle of the nineteenth century the gentry were virtually bi-cultural and bi-lingual even in England: town and country were very different. Metropolitan, middle class authors might mock but the gentry were "rougher" or closer to "their people" when at home, and polished and remote when in town. And when this internal duality declined the very image of gentlemen still carried with it some tolerance, some scepticism, some concern for "one's people", as well as a secure sense of superiority based less on birth than on manners (philistinism, cruel sports and snobbery). The defence of good form was indeed a defence of conventions, not of principles; it was an echo of the empirical and utilitarian approach to politics, including national questions; just as I suspect that the anti-intellectualism of the English governing class, sometimes the pose of anti-intellectualism, had its roots in vague historical memory and fears of what had happened when ideas and confessional beliefs were taken "too seriously", or "out of proportion" in the civil wars in these islands of the seventeenth century.

English historians in the late nineteenth century could not conceal, of course, like American historians of the time, that it was clear that the Anglo-Saxon peoples had a unique capacity for good government, (that is self-government and representative institutions) when they were on their own. In the U.S.A. Mr Dooley remarked that in presidential election years "Celts became honorary Anglo-Saxons". But even these historians, tinged with racial though not racialist doctrines, did not argue a general superiority for the English suddenly became hands-across-the-sea Anglo-Saxons. (How I welcome the Anglo-Irish Treaty; how I dislike the weird, ignorant and insulting, to Scots and Welsh and new immigrants, first name of it). They agree with Matthew Arnold in his celebrated *Lectures on Celtic Literature* that the Celts, if lacking in political tradition, were pre-eminent in lyric poetry, ballads and song. Some of these beliefs still linger as English prejudices long after their real political context has been forgotten, indeed changed - if not quite "changed utterly".

So I argue that it is my fellow English who have to come to terms with themselves, and to ask questions that Welsh, Scottish and Irish writers have been asking for much longer. What are the national characteristics and distinct social-psychological needs? What is distinctive in the culture? And until the English attempt to answer these questions sensibly, the others will somehow, however sincere and interesting, somehow hang in the air. "The owl of Minerva flies at dusk". Just as Thatcher offers a passionate caricature of traditional Englishry (even if her two patrons appear to be King Canute and Adam Smith), some real thought at last begins. In a book that deserved far greater notice, *Englishness: Politics and Culture 1880-1920* (eds. Robert Colls and Phillip Dodd), one of the editors made a profound remark: "Matthew Arnold's ... lectures of the 1860's are a reminder that the definition of the English is inseparable from that of the non-English; Englishness is not so much a category as a relationship,". But what good is for the English goose should be good for the Celtic ganders.

That is why I believe, thinking of Ireland, that while nationalisms are real and authentic in these islands, yet none are as self-sufficient as most of their adepts claim. In Northern Ireland most people are, in fact, torn in two directions: "torn", that is, while their political leaders will not recognise that people can, with dignity, face culturally in two directions at once. Political institutions should be invented to match. In the world before nation states such dualities and pluralities were common enough, as still in some other border areas today. "No man is an island", nor nations as intermingled as ours either. We have not been able to be one people but nor can we ever be fully independent of each other, even politically. We are all inter-independent. Irish, Scottish and Welsh intellectuals have long complained about Anglicisation. But there is less study or appreciation of how much which ever culture one starts with, culture is itself so much a product of the others, and probably the richer for it. Not only intellectuals can live in, or in and out of, two or more cultures. The migrant poor have done it for centuries. But English intellectuals, on the whole, are the last of the four nations to begin to face this squarely. But at least they are ahead of their leading politicians. And that passport, anyway, is to change. And perhaps after 1992 all hotel registers will only ask our nationality if we are not citizens of the European Community, a common citizenship of a kind that will not change national identities as such, but temper their relationships.

34

ON BEING AN ULSTER PROTESTANT

W. HARVEY COX

When I was asked to contribute to this day school on "National Identity in the British Isles", I considered that the simplest and most useful thing to offer was to be myself, and I offered the title above. For whatever reason the title that appeared in the programme, however was "On being a Northern Irish Protestant". The contrast between the two titles is not a bad point at which to start.

For the term "Northern Ireland" is artificial, and only dates back to 1920. It refers to a political arrangement, arrived at in that year in the Government of Ireland Act (which was intended to create two jurisdictions in Ireland, namely Northern Ireland and Southern Ireland). It is an official term; but it has very little emotional resonance. We may be Northern Irish in fact, but that is not a fact to set the pulse beating. It is that we are Ulstermen that carries a weight of reverberations down the centuries and links us with our grandfathers and the "bygone days of yore", in ways that "Northern Ireland" can never do. It was the "Ulster plantation" that created us; it was "Ulster will fight and Ulster will be right" in the anti-Home Rule bill days; it was the 36th Ulster Division that did fight, on the Somme. "Northern Ireland" is for the Tourist Board; "Ulster" is for the heart.

So I chose the term very deliberately. It combines a sense of emotional attachment to a territory and a people with a descriptive precision which no other term possesses.

Of course, Ulster is, strictly speaking, not another term for Northern Ireland, for a third of it is in the Republic. But if I am honest I will admit that the part of Ulster outside Northern Ireland does not count, as far as I am concerned. Of course also, everybody knows that in Ulster there are Catholics as well as Protestants - 50% in the old historic province, 38 - 40% in the six counties of Northern Ireland. As I shall show, their presence is crucial to our identity. But for them, I would venture to suggest, the term Ulster Catholic has a descriptive truth but little resonance, since they have tended (hitherto at least) to identify with Ireland as a whole and only secondarily, if at all, with Ulster, still less with Northern Ireland.

The term "Ulster Protestant" is appropriate not only because nothing else describes what we are, but also because it delineates us with some precision from what we are not. Are we Irish? Yes, but only in a certain sense; there is no doubt that our nineteenth century forebears did think of themselves as Irish. But Irishness came, in the crucial years 1880 - 1920, to be defined by the Irish majority in a way - nationalist, Gaelic, Catholic, that the rest were and are unable to identify with. Are we English? Certainly not. Are we British? Yes, but Britishness doesn't come raw. It comes refined through Englishness, Welshness, Scottishness - or even these days, through Caribbeanness or various forms of Asianness. So we are British, but after our own fashion. One might say that one of the crucial contributions of the Welsh and the Scots, as far as we are concerned, is to show that there are ways of being British without being English (indeed while even being, in varying degrees, anti-English). Besides, we cannot take the risk of being just British. Supposing the English (with the Welsh and Scots), chose to define "British" in a way that excluded us? We couldn't continue to be purely British in a Britain that wanted us to be something else - i.e. Irish. Are we Ulstermen? Yes, but that does not mean that all Ulstermen identify with each other or even, all Belfastmen do so. To take an extreme example, Mr Gerry Adams of Sinn Fein has often written of his love for his and my native city. I can see what he means. Nevertheless, to a Protestant, Adams is someone who lives in the house, unfortunately, but is not part of the family. (In contrast he actually wants Ulster Protestants to regard themselves as part of his family. But he has rather a perverse way of showing it).

Let me remind you of Ernest Geller's definition of a nation, which seems to me to fit the case exactly -

i.   Two men are of the same nation if and only if they share the same culture, where culture in turn means a
        system of ideas and associations and ways of behaving and communicating.

I have to acknowledge that Adams and his IRA colleagues are, in the limited sense I have alluded to, fellow Ulstermen and, for that matter, fellow Irishmen. But though living on the same territory may be, in most cases, a necessary condition for a sense of common nationality, it is certainly not, as Gellner would insist, a sufficient one. On the contrary, what the conflict in Ulster is all about is a clash of national identities, as each side, at least in its most fundamentalist manifestation, struggles to maintain its own perceived national identity against what are perceived to be the efforts of the other to suppress it.

In the Protestant case this takes the form of Unionism, a political position to which all but a few adhere, in one way or another. So much so that "Protestant" and "Unionist" are virtually synonymous. But we need to remember that for two thirds of their existence unionism as we know it today was not of the essence of Ulster Protestantism, and it is not essential, though it is usual, for an Ulster Protestant to be an unionist.

There is no nationality of Ulsterness unlike, say, that of Welshness. A distinguishing feature of Ulster is that neither side there has aspired to become a nation of their own or to have an Ulster state; the much polled people of the province have never shown much support for the idea of independence or separate statehood. On each side the desire is for the territory to continue to be, or to become, part of a larger nation.

So we have, in fact, a very confused situation. We would appear to be a people chiefly characterising ourselves by what we are not, neurotically undecided as to what we actually are. Let me illustrate from personal experience. Someone I know, once played rugby for Ireland. In one sense what could be more Irish than to wear a green shirt at Lansdowne road, cheered by 65,000 fellow Irishmen and women? But because of his job, my friend is an agent of the British state in Northern Ireland, one of a considerable number of people defined by the Provisional IRA as a "legitimate target". By republican lights you can't get more anti-Irish than that. A fairly acute case of the cross-pressure of identities, one would have though. But my friend is not, in any sense, a neurotic man. On the contrary, he appears remarkably free of self-doubt. He knows exactly what he is; he is an Ulster Protestant.

An Ulster Protestant is one a community of some 950,000 people originating in a migration from Scotland and England in the seventeenth century and distinguished from the rest of the peoples of Ireland by that origin and by the religious difference that went with it. Over time, as the Irish majority developed a sense of Irish nationality and a yearning to fulfil this in a state, so the Ulster Protestant sense of distinctiveness developed into a combined sense, both of Britishness and of aversion to what Irishness had come to imply.

Let me attempt to delineate some of the shared characteristics of the Ulster Protestant community. I would sum these up under four heads -

a.   They are "planters"
b.   They are "Protestants"
c.   They are "besieged"
d.   They are uncertain and insecure.

The first two of these relate to the character of the community in itself: the latter two refer to their perceived relationship to, respectively, Ireland as a whole and the United Kingdom.

Irish people of whatever tradition have, in contrast with most of the English, a strong sense of the land. For Ulster Protestants this takes the form of a strongly proprietorial sense about the province. Everywhere in the land of Ulster are to be found the marks put upon it by our planter forebears and by the generations since then. The places bear our names - Jordanstown, Castledawson, Hillsborough, Newtown Hamilton, Brookeborough. The layout of numerous towns and villages, the inheritance of public buildings, reflects still the cosy prosperity the generations subsequent to the planters built up. The countryside, especially of East Ulster, still bears the signs of having been the only part of Ireland to develop industry on any widespread scale. The sons of the planters applied the Protestant ethic to their work and the proof of its superiority was there to see in the burgeoning of industry. The crowning of this was the development of the Belfast industrial area and the jewels in the crown were the great passenger liners, then the greatest in the world, built at Queen's Island from 1890 to 1914. (How ironic that the largest and finest man-made object built in Ireland should have been the Titanic).

There is, then, a strong sense, reflected in many dimensions, from place names to the vivid iconography of the Orange Order, of Ulster Protestants as a community through history, imposing their will upon the land, marking it with the manifold signs of their settlement and their subsequent achievements. Of course, the Catholics of Ulster have been present throughout this history, touching it all along the line. But in a very real sense there are two histories, not one, and the Catholics' one is different.

We now come to religion. As a pair of labels distinguishing two sets of people "Catholic" and "Protestant" are immensely apposite. But they are not mere labels. Ulster Protestants take their Protestantism seriously. Surveys indicate that one third consider themselves regular church-goers It is however, notoriously the case that in Ulster, in a way which has no counterpart in the other parts of the United Kingdom, the religion of Protestantism exists in the context of Catholicism, and is marked by fear and loathing of it. Let me quote from the Laws and Ordinances of the Orange Institution of Ireland, which rather aptly encapsulates the mixture of sincere Christian virtue as interpreted by the Protestant tradition, and strenuous anti- Catholicism.

The Institution is composed of Protestants, united and resolved to the utmost of their power to support and defend the rightful Sovereign, the Protestant religion, the Laws of the real, the Legislative Union, and the Succession to the Throne in the house of Brunswick, BEING PROTESTANT; and united further for the defence of their own Persons and Properties, and the Maintenance of the Public Peace. It is exclusively an Association of those who are attached to the religion of the Reformation, and will not admit into its Brotherhood persons whom an intolerant spirit leads to persecute, injure, or upbroad any man on account of his religious opinions. They associate also in honour of King William III, Prince of Orange, whose name they bear, as supporters of his glorious memory.

An Orangeman should have a sincere love and veneration for his Heavenly Father; an humble and steadfast faith in Jesus Christ, the Saviour of mankind, believing in Him as the only

Mediator between God and Man. He should cultivate truth and justice, brotherly kindness and charity, devotion and piety, concord and unity, and obedience to the laws; his deportment should be gentle and compassionate, kind and courteous; he should seek the society of the virtuous and avoid that of all evil; he should honour and diligently study the Holy Scriptures, and make them the rule of his faith and practice; he should love, uphold, and defend the Protestant religion, and sincerely desire and endeavour to propagate its doctrines and precepts; he should strenuously oppose the fatal errors and doctrines of the Church of Rome, and scrupulously avoid countenancing (by his presence or otherwise) any act or ceremony of Popish Worship; he should, by all lawful means, resist the ascendancy of that Church, its encroachments, and the extension of its power, ever abstaining from all uncharitable words, actions or sentiments towards his Roman Catholic Brethren.

It will be observed that the anti-Catholicism here is couched in civil language and a distinction made between the error of the individual, who is to be respected, and the sin of the institution, which is excoriated. But it cannot be denied that this distinction is not so easily observed in practice by passionate and ill-educated men. Which brings us to Dr. Ian Paisley and his Free Presbyterian Church, a group which, though small in number, has come to express, for outsiders, Ulster Protestantism at its most quintessential and undiluted. This may be, indeed is, unfair. To many in Ulster Paisley is an embarrassment. But in searching for the key to the appeal of Dr. Paisley (who elsewhere in these islands would be dismissed as a theological primitive) one recent academic author, Steve Bruce, has argued that the power of Paisley, especially with the voters, (his party having far more adherents than his church) rests precisely in his articulation of a politico-religious creed, which, in a confusing world, expresses the essence of Ulster Protestantism at its most direct and simple. Where other churchmen speak a universal language, with merely an Ulster accent, Paisley is a uniquely Ulster product; he is inconceivable elsewhere. Hence his powerful appeal to those whose identity is most bound up in their being products of their region - the less educated and most uncosmopolitan.

But the Protestant dimension does not have to be purely a religious one, or indeed religious at all. It can be seen as part of a broader Anglo-American Protestant tradition - rational, democratic and libertarian. One Presbyterian minister describes the ethos of government in his church - "If you were an elder in your church, taking part in the important decisions at the level of the local congregation, the presbytery or the General Assembly, you were not anxious to have political decisions made for you by other people. You made up your own mind, and did not take your orders from anyone; and so your commitment to personal liberty and to democratic processes was very strong". This is not, sadly, a picture familiar to outsiders, but it is there and it is important. It may help to explain why the fact that the Anglo-Irish Agreement was negotiated over their heads without consultation has been so powerfully seen in Ulster as adding insult to injury. And it is, of course, an important element in Ulster Protestant objection to the ways of the Roman Catholic Church in Ireland, an objection shared by Ulster Protestants of all creeds and of none. Here for instance, is the poet John Hewitt, who died, sadly, in 1987 and whose dissenterism took the ultimate form of agnosticism in religion and radicalism in politics:

> I fear their creed, as we have always feared
> The lifted hand against unfettered thought.

It is not our purpose here to assess to what extent this antagonism to Catholicism is justified by reality, or whether, if it ever was, developments over recent years have outmoded it. But we do well to remember that the dislike and disrespect of the two Irish religious traditions for each other was, until recent decades, deep and mutual. As recently as 1931 Cardinal MacRory, the then Roman Catholic Archbishop of Armagh, said that "The Protestant Church in Ireland - and the same is true of the Protestant Church anywhere else - is not only not the rightful representative of the early Irish Church, but it is not even a part of the Church of Christ".

Let me now turn to attitudes to the rest of Ireland and to Britain. Until the development of the Home Rule Movement in the later nineteenth century, there could be no doubt that the Protestants of Ulster regarded themselves as Irish. Unionism, like Protestantism, was seen by them as a way of being Irish. Before it acquired political, separatist connotations, the revival of interest in Gaelic language and culture was pioneered by a number of gentlemen-scholars who were Protestants and Unionists. There was no aversion to the use of Irish for mottoes and slogans by essentially union-supporting institutions such as regiments. All that had changed by 1920. Today, orthodox unionists will so emphasise their Britishness as to deny that they are Irish at all. When Irish nationalists deplore this denial, along with a general refusal to participate in "Irish" (i.e. Gaelic-inspired) culture, on the part of Ulster Protestants, we have to say that in large part this is their fault, for creating for themselves a definition of Irishness which in practice excluded, or relegated to second class Irishness, those who were not Catholic, not anti-British, and did not identify with the Gaelic myth. It was, at least in part, a reaction against this that led some Ulster Protestants into as exaggerated a form of pro-Britishness as their evangelical fundamentalism presented itself as an exaggerated form of Protestantism.

This exclusivist identification of Irishness with the nationalist version of it was enshrined in 1937 in the Irish Constitution, still in operation, which refers in Article Two to "the national territory" as comprising "the whole island of Ireland, its islands and territorial seas" and refers in Article 3 to "the reintegration of the national territory" as a self-evidently desirable fact. Now, what this means to Unionists is that, officially, the Irish Republic regards their politics as illegitimate. Take it in conjunction with Cardinal MacRory's statement and what the Irish majority, in both Church and state, are saying to Ulster Protestants is that their religious beliefs are worthless and they have no right to their politics.

An important symbol of this relationship between Catholic majority and Ulster Protestant minority in Ireland is the seige of Derry. The actual event is, as we know, 300 years old. But as A.T.Q. Stewart has vividly put it, "the important thing about the siege of Derry is that it is still going on". There is still a small and intensely loyalist community within the walls of Derry, surrounded by nationalist Catholics. But today it is the border, perhaps, which better stands for what the walls of Derry stood for in 1689. Ulster Unionist politics is obsessed with security (or rather its inadequacy) and with a strong sense of encirclement by hostile forces - the nationalists and republicans within the gates, the Irish Republic without, the Irish Americans, and of course the various unfriendly forces at work in Britain. What this all makes for is a paranoid politics, an inability to relax. Like the Israelis we have to be constantly on guard, we may win many times but we can only loose once.

42

Finally, there is our relationship to Britain. If our countryside furnishes for us many memorials of the plantation, our cities, and especially Belfast, and our institutions, supply daily reminders of our political allegiance to the United Kingdom. This is especially symbolised in the ubiquity of references to the Crown. This is, of course, at least in part a product of the fact that the great growth of Belfast, and with it of many great public institutions, took place during the reign of Queen Victoria, a reign marked throughout the British world by imperialist fervour and adulation of the monarch, leaving Victoria states, streets, universities, hospitals etc. all over the world. But in no city is this deposit as intense as in Belfast. There are no fewer than 14 thoroughfares commemorating the monarch by name or as queen. By virtue of their location two of the three railway stations formerly did the same. So did the deep water channel at the mouth of the river, the location of the main shipbuilding yard, the university and the main teaching hospital. Five of the most prestigious grammar schools in the province are "royal", the main exhibition hall is the "King's Hall", in the suburb of Balmoral, and we play our international football at Windsor Park.

Britain is the necessary protector. At times this dependency upon Britain is bound to look like clinging to mother; and it appears peculiarly distasteful to British observers that it is accompanied by an apparent lack of gratitude which takes the form of refusal to do what mother wants in return. Ulster Protestants appear to be British, but only on their own terms. There can be no doubt that, as David Miller has graphically put it, Ulster loyalism is "conditional loyalism". It is perfectly illustrated by the Orange Order's loyalty to the Crown BEING PROTESTANT. That is, the Crown is offered intense loyalty, but in return for fulfillment of a contractual obligation to be loyal to the loyalists. The dismay in Britain at the niggardly, suspicious politics this produces is understandable, and there is a longing to call it to account. Decide what it is you are loyal to. But consider the implication of this. The Ulster people cannot be unconditionally loyal to a state which could cut them off without a penny, deliver them into the hands of their perceived enemies. The only thing that would secure unconditional loyalty would be an unconditional guarantee of support and protection given in a believable form, and this cannot be supplied. (Though in successive declarations Parliament has, in fact, gone as far as any Parliament can in this direction.)

43

That is why the Anglo-Irish Agreement of November 1985 delivered such a deep shock and, for many, confirmed their worst suspicions of Britain. That Britain and the Republic should act as mutual friends where Ulster loyalists see the latter as, essentially, an enemy, turns the world upside down.

Now there are of course many divisions among the 950,00 Protestants. These divisions of class, denomination, religious versus non-religious, town versus country are all important, but, as the response to the Agreement showed, there is a great unanimity or bonding together in times of crises. All this stems from our origins as a colony, planted on alien soil, holding it against natives considered hostile and backward, molding it, merging with it and in the process acquiring a certain toughness or even bloodymindedness. But it is a colony of over 350 years, older than those of America or Australia or white South Africa. Like the Americans and Australians, we would have founded a nation in Ireland if the native Irish hadn't been there already. Indeed to a certain degree, in the late eighteenth century we did.

It has often been argued that much of the character of Ulster Protestantism is marked by a hardness and an insecurity, flowing from the community's origin as a planted colony. One could certainly argue that, with their political future more uncertain now than ever, they have more grounds for insecurity too than ever. The Ulster Protestant is by so means an endangered species, but Ulster Unionism, with which that identity is strongly bound up, could be an endangered cause. The key to peace in Ireland rests in finding means whereby both the communities of Ulster can live, each secure in their identity and free from threats to their future. This can only mean some modification of the way that identity has been expressed politically, on the part of one, or other, or both groups. This is extremely tricky since both are the product of three hundred years of conflict and the growth of mutually incompatible political objectives. In my view the way out must be through a greater actualisation of a pluralism of identity and political expression of it throughout the British Isles. Since that is what I assume the Anglo-Irish agreement to be about, at least in principle, if not in the manner of negotiation and implementation, I hold it to be a right development.

John Hewitt, whom I quoted earlier, has a well-known poem, "The Colony", which describes the situation of the Romans in Britain some generations after their arrival. They have created a society. They have not "gone native" but they are no longer metropolitan Romans either. Rome, indeed, is remote from their lives and has its own concerns. The colony needs, feels it has earned, a secure future in the land it has made its own. There can be doubt of whom Hewitt is really speaking. He

would make amends by fraternising, by small friendly gestures,

hoping by patient words I may convince

my people and this people we are changed

from the raw levies which usurped the land,

if not to kin, to co-inhabitants,

as goat and ox may graze in the same field

and each gain something from proximity;

for we have rights drawn from the soil and sky;

the use, the pace, the patient years of labour,

the rain against the lips, the changing light,

the heavy clay-sucked stride, have altered us;

we would be strangers in the Capitol;

this is our country also, no-where else;

and we shall not be outcast on the world.

THE DYNAMIC OF WELSH IDENTITY

EMYR W. WILLIAMS

In considering issues of national identity, it must initially be recognised that the crucial factor is not that of "what identities exist" but rather that of "why and how they enter the "political arena". We are dealing with the "politics of identity" a reality revealed from the most superficial consideration of national identities in Britain. Thus whilst the existence of Welsh, English, Scottish and Irish identities can be seen as complementary, the existence of an alternative overlapping British identity, highlights both the ideological nature of identity and the potential for conflict.

We also live in a context in which identities are in flux, for not only does Britain's entry into the European Community lay the foundations for a new Western European identity, but also the material bases of British nationalism are being removed, in turn granting a new relevance to Welsh and Scottish identities. These departures highlight the fact that, developing an understanding of the politics of identity is not simply an empirical matter, but rather is a theoretical issue demanding a clear and explicit framework. My aim initially in this paper will be to address relevant theoretical problems, before proceeding briefly to consider issues relating to British identity and subsequently focusing at greater length on the Welsh dimension.

The framework set out by Marx in the 1859 preface, in my experience, provides the only theory remotely capable of offering an insight into the complexity which we seek to understand; it is relevant to remind ourselves of the foundations of his analysis. He states that:

> In the social production of their existence, men inevitably enter into definite relations, which are independent of their will, namely relations of production appropriate to a given stage in the development of their material forces of production. The totality of these relations of production constitute the economic structure of society, the real foundations, on which arises a legal and political superstructure and to which correspond definite forms of social consciousness. The mode of production of material life conditions the general process of social, political and intellectual life.

This is, of course, an essentially deterministic model, which conceives of the economic structure as the motive force of history, conditioning the relatively autonomous spheres of social and intellectual life, as well as the nature of the legal and political superstructure. Recognition of the determinism of that economic base is essential if we are to understand the complexity of the contemporary context. It is also necessary to locate national ideologies (which provide a basis for political identity) within his framework.

It is possible to identify two kinds of ideology within social and intellectual life, these being either class ideologies or national ideologies. Within twentieth century Britain national ideologies have been of two main kinds. On the one hand the central state (or political superstructure) has been used by various elites to promote a British nationalism; alternatively at the level of the civil society the historic ethnic composition of Britain has provided a basis for Welsh, English, Irish and Scottish nationalism. **What is of particular interest is that these national ideologies enter the political stage not in isolation, but already integrated into various class ideologies in an active role of mobilisation and struggle.** Indeed I wish to argue that such an ideological synthesis will in fact reflect both the changing inter-relationship of classes, and the changing relative position of a country within the broader world system. The concept of national ideologies and thus national identities as entailing a dynamic is thus entirely appropriate.

It is also essential to recognise that the three basic dimensions set out by Marx in the 1859 preface, in practice influence each other. Social and intellectual life will influence the nature of the political superstructure; the political superstructure will influence social and intellectual life. Both in their turn will influence the economic structure. What is crucial to this model is a concept of the economic structure as ultimately constituting the determining aspect in relation to which the other aspects experience only a relative autonomy.

Part of the difficulty of comprehending the existence of the dynamic of identity emanates from the seeming permanence of current ideological orthodoxy. It is only careful historical analysis that can reveal these shifts. Thus it seems that the dominant 19th century concept of social formation in which we live, was that of the United Kingdom - an entity which was seen as being composed of three nationalities, the English, Scots and Irish with a fourth nationality - the Welsh - gaining recognition around 1886. However during the closing decades of the century as the military and commercial position of the United Kingdom weakened within the wider world system, increased political intervention became a necessity, enabling the ruling class to increase its relative political autonomy and to generate a British nationalism. In turn the development of the Welfare State and ultimately the evolution of a consensus politics provided a broader material underpinning for this nationalism and created a framework within which all British parties could operate. The primary class interest represented within British nationalism was in this way camouflaged though the dismantling of that nationalism following the 1979 election revealed the identity of these forces. Many of the contemporary difficulties experienced by the Labour Party stem from the belief of its leadership that British nationalism (and the benefits which accrued to the working class from it) entail a need to defend that form of politics rather than proceeding to develop a radical alternative.

In reality the existence of a British nationalism, and a British identity promoted by the ruling elite thus marked an era of transition in the history of the United Kingdom. This entailed a shift from the unchallenged world military and commercial supremacy of the latter half of the 19th century, to absorption into a Western European State in the closing decades of the 20th century.

Whilst the changing relative position of the UK within the world system provides the key to understanding the parameters of British nationalism, in Welsh nationalism we are confronted by a politics having a significantly different dynamic. Not only is one class far more visibly identified with at least the initial stages of this nationalism, but also the success of marginal elements in establishing the dominant definition of Welsh identity has to be noted. My aim will be to trace the synthesis of class ideology and national ideology found within modern Welsh nationalism, to consider the manner in which this politics has reflected the changing relationship of classes within Welsh society, and the varying capacity of the central state to exercise hegemony over Wales. In a concluding section the adequacy of the dominant nationalist definition of Welshness to the present historical context will be assessed.

The key creative phase in the development of modern Welsh nationalism occurred during the 19th century, but the 20th century has been characterised by reaction to change and an attempt to conserve and re-mobilize. Three distinct phases can be identified in the process which culminated in the development of a Welsh nationalism at the turn of the century. Within the wider British context a non-conformist free trade outlook evolved, at first as a minority perspective. It established its dominance in Wales at the election of 1880, and subsequently there was a transition from a U.K. perspective to a radical Welsh perspective.

Until the opening decades of the 19th century, the theology of old dissent had been tailored to the specific needs of a "petit - bourgeoisie" who could conceive of themselves as the "elect". This ideology did not offer itself as a means of advance for other social groups, and did it appears that old dissent as yet did not aspire to a broader social role. However as the industrial revolution gathered momentum, dissenting theology was re-theorised in order to render is capable of serving broader social forces. That re-theorisation was complemented by the integration of other dimension in particular utilitarian philosophy and Manchester economics. By the mid 1840s there had thus developed a relatively mature radical Nonconformist perspective, which was rapidly eroding the dominance of the Anglican Church and the Whig-Tory ruling class within Welsh civil society. At the same time the increasingly rapid development of the forces of production entailed in the industrial revolution, created severe tensions within the Anglican *bloc* ultimately leading Methodism in Wales to align itself with nonconformity. The radicals were thus gaining the ascendancy.

Despite the changing balance of social forces in Wales, the nonconformist free-traders made little impression within the sphere of formal politics, for until the 1867 Reform Act they were largely excluded from the electoral process. However the Reform Act laid the foundations for a political transformation ultimately accomplished at the election of 1880. At that point the nonconformists emerged as the dominant political force in Wales, not only establishing control over the Liberal Party but also inaugurating 40 years of Liberal domination of politics in Wales. The election of 1880 developed nonconformity into a Liberal nonconformity and created Liberal nonconformist Wales.

The implications of this departure were initially ambiguous for victory was at first interpreted from an UK perspective. The regionalised nature in the UK, however, implied that grave difficulties were entailed in any attempt to meet Liberal nonconformist aspirations on the basis of legislation which was to apply uniformly throughout Britain. It thus became necessary to proceed further with the process of legislating separately for the specific regions and nations of Britain. In relation to Wales the passing of the Welsh Sunday Closing Act of 1881 became the initial instance in this process. It must be stressed that this departure did not imply recognition of Welsh nationalism, but rather constituted a pragmatic attempt to accommodate new radical aspirations. There is much to suggest that up to 1886 the ruling class did not even recognise the existence of a distinct Welsh nation, and that it was the Irish crisis of 1885-86 which led Gladstone to re-examine his assumptions. However his recognition of Welsh nationality in 1886 created an explicit framework whereby concessions could be made to Liberal nonconformity in Wales by the Anglican ruling class. Recognition of Welsh nationality thus became a way out of a political *impasse* for both Liberal nonconformity in Wales and the leadership of the Liberal Party. Subsequently Liberal nonconformist demands in relation to such issues as disestablishment and education became the defining characteristics of Welsh politics.

By the early 1880s the radical nonconformists has thus not only succeeded in developing a relatively mature world view, but had also established their own electoral preponderance - in the process smashing the Whig-Tory political hegemony in Wales. In turn this latter development created a major challenge for Liberal nonconformity for they needed to establish their own political hegemony in Wales. This, in effect, constituted a new departure in Welsh politics. As the 1880s advanced the accession of an Oxbridge-educated intelligentsia into the Liberal Party provided the means for solving this problem, but at first it was unclear what path events would follow.

The new intellectuals, having been drawn from Welsh Liberal nonconformity, had of course been educated in the perspectives of a ruling class. On returning to Wales during the mid 1880s they began to elaborate a Welsh nationalist outlook. From early 1886 this assumed the form of Tom Ellis' radical Welsh Home rule movement, Cymru Fydd. The dynamic of Liberal nonconformist politics however pointed in another direction. Essentially the Local Government Act of 1888 which created the new County Councils entailed the culmination of a process of transforming these social forces from being socially subordinate to being a local establishment having conservative interests. The demand for the disestablishment of the Church remained a key aspiration, but hardly one which determined the nature of their social outlook. The County Council elections of 1889, which resulted in the Liberals securing 390 of the 590 seats in Wales, thus presaged the development of an alternative nationalism to that being elaborated by Tom Ellis. In the early 1890s there emerged a romantic cultural nationalism which in effect constituted the crowning glory of Liberal nonconformist politics. In this context at least some of the Oxbridge intelligentsia realigned their political careers. Indicative of this process is O. M. Edwards, who had been active in Tom Ellis's Home Rule movement and now assumed the literary role for which he is best remembered.

From the early 1890s Liberal nonconformists developed into a Liberal Nonconformist Welsh nationalism, and this was the form assumed by the Liberal hegemony in Wales through until 1922. It must be stressed that this nationalism had no significant constitutional aspirations in relation to Wales. It was not a Home Rule politics, for essentially Liberal individualism and free trade ideology negated any such concept. Rather this politics was a celebration of the accomplishments of Liberal nonconformist Wales within the broader context of the United Kingdom and Empire. By contrast the Cymru Fydd Home Rule movement which had emerged in 1886 was a very marginal phenomenon. It was a form of politics which experienced a temporary popularity during the mid 1890s but subsequently the growth of British nationalism confined the basis of its appeal. However a limited movement did survive through until 1926, initially in the Liberal Party and subsequently within the Labour Party.

51

Meanwhile from the turn of the century, Liberal nonconformist Welsh Nationalism was confronted by two major challenges. On the one hand the increasing polarisation of labour and capital was threatening the unity of Liberalism, whilst on the other the growing centralisation of power and the growth of British nationalism posed a broader threat. This latter aspect did not emerge as a major issue until the elaboration of new centralist cultural institutions during the late 1920's. However the crises of Liberalism in Wales rapidly crystalised during 1921 and 1922, for increasing working class militancy and the growing popularity of the Labour Party caught a fragmented Liberal Party in a no man's land. With radical Liberals already moving into the Labour Party, and with capital seeking shelter within the Tory Party the Liberal intellectuals were isolated. In that context the Liberal nonconformist Welsh nationalist hegemony collapsed and Welsh politics reached another turning point. The implications of these developments demand careful analysis.

Firstly, 1922 constituted a crucial turning point at which Liberal nonconformity - aspects of which were already in a decade's long decline - ceased to be the natural dominant cultural expression of the people of Wales. That transition is marked by a shift in the manner in which that culture was conceptualised. Prior to 1922 there was a concept of the culture expressing Welsh aspirations. Subsequently its fossilisation is indicated by the emergence of a concept of the culture as being traditional. Secondly, because the cultural hegemony had collapsed, and thus lost its popular support, broad issues came to the fore. These concerned the adequacy of Liberal Welsh nonconformity as a culture, as against a socialist perspective. For a militant faction of intellectuals the securing of national institutions to impose a revamped Liberal nonconformist nationalism on the people of Wales became a priority. The crisis of 1922 thus generated a nationalist political reaction to the rise of socialism in Wales. This bore broader implications regarding the complexion of Welsh constitutional politics.

In the period from 1886 to 1926, the Cymru Fydd Home Rule tradition been a radical tradition whose outlook initially reflected radical Liberal interests and subsequently radical Labour interests. However following the events of 1922, the Liberal nonconformist nationalists firstly contributed to undermining the Cymru Fydd Home Rule tradition and then established a party of their own - Plaid Genedlaethol Cymru- which in due course emerged as the dominant expression of constitutional politics in Wales. Within the new movement the Cymru Fydd Home Rule tradition was accommodated as a subordinate theme.

The years from 1922 to the early 1930s proved to be a period of transition for those leading intellectuals who established Plaid Genedlaethol Cymru. Having established the party their immediate aim was to secure a rapid political remobilisation of Liberal nonconformity in order to win from the United Kingdom establishment those institutional supports necessary to entrench a re-modelled Liberal nonconformist Welsh Nationalism. In practice they failed to achieve that objective, for the Caernarfon election of 1929 demonstrated their weakness rather than their strength. In turn this failure permitted the Home Rulers to emerge to the fore and re-define the aims of the party in radical terms.

However the nationalist intellectuals deeply entrenched within the party, having lost the battle over aims, were well placed to ensure that the substance of Plaid's politics reflected their own priorities. Moreover during the early 1930s as they recognised that their cultural structure had to be re-theorised and rebuilt, rather than simply reformed and revised, an attempt was made to develop a philosophy and a view of Welsh history. This strategy was initially pursued by Saunders Lewis whilst subsequently a more orthodox vision was developed by Gwynfor Evans.

This pattern of radical constitutional objectives, co-existing within a "conservative" cultural framework, established the pattern of Plaid politics through to 1979. Whether this was a fact of real political significance is open to question, for it can be argued that the party's political identity was largely determined by the broader context in which it operated. From the late 1920's Plaid Genedlaethol Cymru was operating in a context in which the British establishment was attempting to deny the existence of a Welsh identity, and to impose a British identity on Wales. This approach pursued in particular by the BBC sent shock-waves through Welsh political life, drawing condemnation from such prominent figures as David Lloyd George. It also enabled Plaid Genedlaethol Cymru to emerge as the defender of Wales and Welshness against the strategies being pursued by the British political elite. Even Lloyd George was greatly impressed by the performance of Saunders Lewis in challenging the BBC establishment.

Plaid Genedlaethol Cymru, by challenging the attempt to impose a British identity on Wales, forced an accommodation which entailed the creation of a subordinate niche for a Welsh identity within the dominant British nationalist ideology of the state. This initial departure in turn created the foundations for a longer term strategy, for having created a niche for Welsh identity political advance entailed the broadening of that enclave and rolling back the frontiers of Britishness in Wales. The Party's achievements over the period extending to 1979 were remarkable, for Plaid contributed to a process of establishing new national institutions. These initially related to the cultural sphere but subsequently advanced to the sphere of formal politics, the administration of the state and forms of economic intervention in Wales. As a consequence, the process of establishing a range of new Welsh national institutions initiated during the Liberal era (University of Wales, National Library, National Museum, Royal Commission on Ancient Monuments) experienced a renewal from the mid 1930s after having been in abeyance during the previous twenty years.

A phase extending to 1964, saw the establishment of a distinct service for Wales by the BBC in July 1937, the founding of The Welsh Folk Museum at Sain Ffagan in 1946, and the establishment of the Council for Wales and Monmouth in 1948, followed in 1951 by the Ministry for Welsh Affairs. This process culminated in the establishment of the Welsh Office in 1964, a departure which gave a new dimension to the process of institutional development in Wales. Whereas previously that process had entailed the establishment of isolated national bodies, the founding of the Welsh Office entailed the emergence of a separate department of state which rapidly developed a momentum of its own. The extent to which its responsibilities broadened by the mid 1980's will be considered briefly later in this analysis.

In turn 1964 marked a point of departure for a new phase characterised by the accretion of responsibilities within the Welsh Office and the continued establishment of a new national institutions in Wales. This latter aspect in 1969 entailed the creation of the Wales Tourist Board, followed in 1971 by the Sports Council for Wales. Subsequently in 1975 the Land Authority for Wales was established, followed in 1976 by the Welsh Development Agency, and the development Board for Rural Wales in 1977. Whilst these advances succeeded in further broadening the Welsh niche within Britishness from the cultural sphere to the economic sphere, and created an all-Wales politics, it also bore broader implications. Gwynfor Evans' victory at the Carmarthen by-election of July 1966 not only placed the establishment of Welsh democracy on the political agenda, but also rendered the nature of the party's political programme a relevant public issue. Success was transforming Plaid Cymru from being a cultural and economic pressure group for a Wales marginalised by British nationalism, into a potential government of a democratic Welsh State. The young technocrats within the movement not only recognised this new reality, but also tuned into it brilliantly, for in the Wilsonian era of economic planning they produced an economic plan for Wales. This undertaking which was consciously intended to demonstrate that they were a more competent governing elite than anything the British system could generate. Yet there was no attempt to address critically the cultural dimension to the party's programme. On the contrary it was only in the post 1966 period that the cultural strategy developed during the 1920's and 30's reached maturity. It is necessary at this point again to assess the development of the party during its formative years.

Initially it must be recalled that the establishment of Plaid Genedlaethol Cymru was intimately related to the collapse of the Liberal nonconformist Welsh nationalist hegemony in 1922. With that cultural-political edifice having lost its popular support, the first option pursued was that of seeking political institutions to sustain it and impose it on the population of Wales. However the vote secured by the Plaid candidate at the 1929 election demonstrated the party's electoral weakness, and thus the impossibility of coming to an understanding with their colleagues within the British establishment regarding the founding of relevant institutions in Wales. The response of the cultural leadership of the party to this political failure was to create an ideological bastion in order to survive within British nationalism and to withstand the processes of social change confronting them. The Welsh speaking Liberal

55

nonconformist nationalist identity was thus presented as the inherently Welsh identity. Welsh history was appropriated to confirm this model and indeed on the cultural front a wholesale process of reviving cultural forms to create a national tradition centred on Liberal nonconformity was pursued.

Of course this politics did not relate to the political agenda defined by British nationalist politics, and thus techniques of thrusting it on that agenda had to be developed - the burning of the bombing school in 1936 initiating this strategy. As British nationalism receded the new Welsh nationalism could in turn become more liberal and its interventions more hegemonic. This explains the contrast between Saunders Lewis and Gwynfor Evans. The ideological development of this nationalism ultimately reached its conclusion with the publication of Aros Mae by Gwynfor Evans in 1971 - a fascinating book and major intellectual achievement constituting a coherent attempt by liberal nonconformist Welsh nationalism to appropriate Welsh history.

The major practical problem was that this fundamentalist attempt to define Welshness left no room for those excluded from the definition. These issues come to the force in the run up to the 1979 devolution referendum. The manner of Plaid Cymru's growth in itself posed problems, for the movement had grown by recruiting into itself in a corporatist manner, rather than by intervening hegemonically to shift public opinion. In the run-up to the referendum this implied that large swathes of the Welsh electorate not only lacked a clear conception of the role of the proposed Welsh Assembly, but also were deeply suspicious of the real objectives of Plaid Cymru. The issues at stake at the referendum from the public perspective could thus be very different from those defined within formal politics. In that situation the crucial issue in the public mind shifted from support for, or rejection of, a Welsh Assembly having very limited power, to entirely different concerns. These revolved around the question of whether Plaid Cymru's liberal nonconformist Welsh nationalism was to be permitted to secure additional institutional support which could possibly allow it to be imposed on the broader population of Wales.

Very real suspicions that such a departure was possible of course produced an over whelming rejection of the proposals. The conclusions are quite clear, namely that the nationalism dominant within Plaid Cymru from the early 1930s was incapable of uniting the people of Wales in favour of the establishment of a real democratic Welsh politics. Yet it must be recognised that 1979 constituted a crises of success for Plaid Cymru, for it was the party's success in broadening the cultural niche established within British nationalism during the early 30s, that made the founding of an Assembly into a practical political issue. The real problem for Plaid was how it could advance beyond the position secured in the run-up to the 1979 referendum. Neither the Liberal nonconformist nationalists nor the technocrats recognised the impending crises, and both were incapable of transcending the weakness inherent in their own politics.

In practice the devolution referendum of 1979 constituted a subordinate theme in politics and in consequence its long term implications were extremely limited. Not unexpectedly the real dynamics of Welsh identity during the past decade were to be understood in relation to the broader dynamic of British politics. In essence 1979 marked a major turning point in British history, for, with the forces of production having outgrown the political superstructure (thus leading to the absorption of Britain into a new Western European state) long established patterns of intervention which have sustained British nationalism were abandoned.

Thatcherism was an attempt to withdraw the state from a range of interventions within broader society, and subject the factors of production - land, labour and capital, to market forces. Moreover at the same time new forms of inventions were being developed in order to promote the success of the private sector. This latter aspect entailed the establishment of new Welsh institutions; led to an increase in the responsibilities of the Welsh Office and has witnessed successive Welsh secretaries of State assuming a key role in developing strategies aimed at promoting Welsh economic regeneration. Thus, despite the outcome of the 1979 referendum the development of the Welsh State has subsequently gathered momentum. How then do we interpret these developments?

It can be argued that 1979 marked a turning point at which it became necessary to abandon the degree of political intervention required in order to sustain British nationalism. As a consequence we are now moving to a pattern of identities within the United Kingdom broadly similar to that which existed during the 19th century, but with two important differences. Not only will the situation demand a regionalised pattern of economic intervention within England, and the continued elaboration of state structures in Wales and Scotland, but also the development of the European Community implies that a new European identity is capable of emerging. In Wales we are thus moving away from a context of conflict between British and Welsh nationalism, to a situation in which Welsh identity can be both an ethnic identity and a state identity within the evolving parameters of the United Kingdom and the Western European State.

In this paper I have attempted to trace the development of Welsh nationalist politics and to highlight the concept of Welsh identity it sustained. In closing it has to be recognised that the political mobilization it entailed has contributed to a major transformation in Welsh politics, for by now the Welsh state exists, employing around 2,300 civil servants within the Welsh Office itself, with a further 1,500 being employed in subordinate national institutions. During the financial year 1988-9 the Secretary of State for Wales administered a budget of £3,500 million. It is apparent that we are living in a new European Wales, in which the Welsh dimension is in the process of being re-asserted. The basic issue now is whether that Welsh state can be harnessed to the task of economic and cultural regeneration on a democratic basis, in turn contributing to the creation of a new Welsh European identity appropriate to the 21st century.

It is abundantly apparent that a fossilized liberal nonconformist Welsh nationalism with its fixed concept of Welsh identity is incapable of contributing to that process. Indeed the very deliberate attempt to create tunnel vision within large swathes of the Welsh speaking intelligentsia by now constitutes a very negative aspect of the Welsh political process. In essence it inhibits the appropriate articulation of the linguistic and economic dimensions into Welsh Life, in a manner capable of securing advance in relation to both aspects. Whilst recognizing the contribution of Liberal nonconformity to Welsh life and drawing relevant lessons from that experience, the national movement must now quite explicitly recognize the weakness entailed in that ideological synthesis of Liberal nonconformist Welsh nationalism, and acknowledge that it is engaged in developing a new Welsh politics which will in due course generate a new Welsh identity. In developing such politics it must be recognized that there are no easy answers to be drawn either from Karl Marx or Adam Smith; from Saunders Lewis or Gwynfor Evans. The challenge is to understand the current context and to articulate a relevant Welsh dimension into that context. Given such an approach there can be both a genuine optimism of the intellect and an optimism of the will, in relation to the future of Wales.

GOGS, CARDIS AND HWNTWS: REGIONS, NATION AND STATE IN WALES, 1840-1940

NEIL EVANS

It is necessary to begin by explaining my title. It refers to the strong regional identities which exist in Wales; the people of the north, of Cardiganshire, and the south, respectively. The terms are not innocent ones, and can give offence. The first version of this talk was given in Belfast in 1986 and when I told a friend the title he remarked that it was just as well I was giving it in Belfast! What I want to discuss, is the kind of identities which existed in Wales in my chosen century. To what extent did local loyalties give way to Welsh ones or even British ones? I was moved to think about this by Eugen Weber's book, *Peasants into Frenchmen: The Modernisation of Rural France, 1870-1914*. In that he argues that in the course of those forty four years the peasantry entered the modern world. Their prime loyalty became to the state, and not to the *pays* of their birth. They began to look at the world rationally- most graphically illustrated in their declining belief in religion when they found that phosphate fertiliser was more efficatious than having the priest bless the crop. What changed France was state education, military service, roads and railways, and the market economy which they helped to create. By 1914 the peasants were participating fully in French national politics and the enthusiasm with which they went off to defend France in 1914 was an indication of how total the process was. What I wanted to know was did anything like this happen to Welsh people? And, if so, did they become predominantly Welsh or British in the process?

It is easy to detect the kind of local loyalties that existed in Wales before the industrial revolution. It is a myth, of course, that people stayed within the parish of their birth, but studies done of the mid-nineteenth century show that the great bulk of people in rural Wales lived in the county of their birth, and usually within a fairly small portion of it. Contacts with the wider world were fleeting and often hostile. One *Cardi* recalled how he had gone to Knighton and aroused the suspicion of the shopkeeper who thought he was passing fraudalent coin. He became so busy testing it that he didn't notice that the wily Cardi had picked it up from his own counter and proceded to pay the man with his own money! The real joke comes later.

Of course I should [have confessed to the shopkeeper] at Tregaron or Aberystwyth, but the *Saeson* have taken a good deal from us, they have not given us back yet. [Would he have done this in Carmarthen, pressed his questioner] Oh yes; I owe the 'whelps' a deeper grudge than I owe the *Saeson*. I was once badly thrashed at Llandovery Fair and I am still in their debt.

His use of a local nickname was quite typical of the period. We can find Ruthin 'cats', 'one a wanting' from Llanilltud Fawr in Glamorgan and 'the Black Army' from Llantrisant, amongst a host of others. The festivals of the *Gwyl Mabsant*, powerfully analysed by Richard Suggett in a previous dayschool, show the same deeply attached and militant localism. Anyone washed up on the shores of Wales after a shipwreck felt the weight of the predatory instinct towards strangers, and vagrants were convenient scapegoats for local crime.

How did industrialisation affect this? In France, with its dominating capital, and its vast peasant population (*Paris and the French Desert*, is the title of one study) more easily lends itself to Weber's approach than does Wales. In Wales extensive industrialisation was very unevenly spread between the regions. South Wales became one of the success stories of British capitalism. Population became increasingly concentrated there. In 1801 Glamorgan and Monmouthshire held 20% of the population of Wales; in 1851 33% and in 1911 63%. North west Wales, the land of the *gog* shared a limited amount of this. Tom Jones was making an ideological point when he remarked that it was more balanced than south Wales, having not only industry, but agriculture and rich visitors too, yet at the same time he was also capturing the social reality. The rest of north Wales with its coalfield in the east and its resorts on the north coast shared in the new industrial world. The problems seemed to come in the middle- for *Cardis* in particular, but for that wider region of the 'Welsh desert' of mid-Wales too. Here modern industry had passed them by and rural industries were succumbing to competition from elsewhere. Their viability as communities seemed to be threatened. South Cardiganshire showed the crisis at its starkest. In the 1880s J.E. Vincent said it was the area of Wales least known to visitors. Its lead mines had already collapsed and with them the coastal shipping that had once been its lifeline. A guide book published in 1895 to attract in visitors only succeeded in showing the area's isolation (though it did emphasise the bravery of local people in rescuing people from shipwrecks- some things had already changed!). In 1919 it was being complained that Cardiganshire was 'almost locked up', its transport was so bad and that Newquay was like a stranded ship. It cost 7/- a ton to take coal from Cardiff to Bombay, and £1 to take it 7 miles inland from Newquay. In desperation people looked to light railways (subsidised by County Councils under the Light Railways Act of 1896) for the salvation of their district. When the Lampeter to Aberaeron line opened in May 1911, newspapers proclaimed 'WEST WALES OPENED UP BY RAILWAY ENTERPRISE' and one local worthy became completely carried away by the occasion; 'not only would the rateable value of the county be increased, but the country in question would be opened up and be in direct communication with Aberystwyth and North Wales. When the railway was built Talley would be found to be one of the finest inland watering places in Wales'. The tensions of this area helped generate the religious revival of 1904-5 and the reaction of its people launched Caradoc Evans's bitter satires on rural nonconformity.

The sense of desperation was less intense elsewhere in rural Wales, but it clearly existed. There were many light railway projects in which hope was more prominent than the prospect of a real economic return. Schemes to turn Abersoch into a major resort were canvassed; in 1895 the Faenol Estate finally allowed the building of the Snowdon Mountain Railway. Many feared that life on the land was unattractive. The Welsh Industries Association was launched in 1899 in an attempt to develop cottage industries to staunch the flow to the towns. Lady St. David's created a village society in Pembrokeshire with the aim of relieving monotony and dullness, and bringing to the smallest village the spirit of the National Eisteddfod and the Cymmrodorion Society. Tom Ellis complained to the Land Commission in 1893 of the lack of village halls and public libraries in Merioneth. Contact with industrial areas was clearly raising the stakes in rural Wales. The Rev. Richard Hughes asked 'How can the dwellers in the country districts so use the forces that are at work in our modern life, so to raise themselves to the full exercise of the responsibilities, privileges and blessings of citizenship?' Much was hoped for from the parish councils of 1894, to restore life through local democracy. Village institutes and village halls began to spread after the turn of the century.

This may have seemed like a diversion, but it was made in order to raise the issue of the extent of integration in nineteenth-century Wales. Was it possible for there to be a sense of unity when economic divides were perceived to be so wide? Was Wales simply an unresolved series of conflicts between *Gogs*, *Cardis* and the *Hwntws* who were gathering all the wealth to themselves? I think not. There were, until after the turn of the century, much stronger binding forces than this rift over the unevenness of development.

The most important of these was religion. Nonconformity was divided into a host of competing sects and denominations, but they had more in common than divided them. All were primitive in their style and Calvinist in theology; they were united by their opposition to the Church of England. By the end of the nineteenth century a denominational structure linked people in the north with those in the south. Independents and Baptists were stronger in the south than in the north, and the opposite applied to Calvinistic Methodists, but each donomination had a presence throughout Wales. They were united by a language and language ensured that their theological discussion remained locked in a 17th century time warp. Not for them the confrontation with evolutionism; ignoring it was part of what made a Welsh nonconformist a Welsh nonconformist rather than an English one.

Language was also a uniting bond. It was still spoken by more than half the population in 1891, and more importantly it would be hard to make a clear linguistic division between rural and industrial areas at that time. John Southall's map of its distribution in 1891 shows it as strongly entrenched in the Rhondda Valleys and in the industrial areas to the west of that Welsh Klondike.

This shading of the language zones was the product of the pattern of migration in nineteenth-century Wales. The bulk of the movement was within the borders of Wales, and this meant that the family links between rural and industrial Wales were strong ones. In 1868 droves of voters went from Merthyr to Cardiganshire to exercise their right to vote in the election. Dylan Thomas's visits to Fernhill were a late expression of one of the key phenomena of Welsh industrialisation.

All these things were expressed in the quite remarkable political unity of late nineteenth century Wales. The Liberals secured a clear majority in 1868; in 1906 the Tories did not take a single seat. Usually, they had four. Even in the year of Liberal disasters of 1895 the Tories got only eight.

Underlying much of this was the growth of communications. In the 1860s railways penetrated the Welsh interior and moved away from their coastal origins and moorings. Forty per cent of the mileage laid down in Wales was put down in that decade. The emergence of the Cambrian Coast and Mid-Wales lines created a ramshakle system. It has been observed that the network in rural Wales was dense in relation to its population. Dai Smith comments, 'There were countries without maps but no nations...without railways.' The railway network spread the message. From Carmarthen, Denbigh, Aberdare and Caernarfon a flood of publications were distributed. In the 1880s according to Beriah Gwynfe Evans there were 17 Welsh language weekly papers with a combined circulation of 120,000. In addition 150,000 copies of monthly publications were sold, and the annual value of all Welsh literature sold was estimated at £200,000. The Eisteddfod became a national institution by its adroit use of these new lines of communication. The regions of Wales were in many ways unified by their sense of competing for superiority. This is the *Caernarfon and Denbigh Herald* in 1886;

> There was a brass band contest the other day at Merthyr; and the bandsmen of North Wales will learn with interest that one of the Cardiff journals admits without any circumlocution that the brass bands of the southern districts are far behind those of the north. It is said to be 'very evident that before the local bands can attain equality with the bands of the north, more attention must be paid to the condition and tone of the instruments'. Of course this quotation suggests the old proverb that 'the bad workman always complains of his tools' and our local bands will be ready to meet in friendly rivalry with their southern bretheren even when all deficiencies in 'condition and tone' of their instruments have been made good.

Victory was not only sweet, but integrating.

How was Wales integrated into the British state? It is usually (and rightly) stressed that Wales fitted neatly into the British state. The arguments of Welsh liberals were essentially arguments for more recognition within that structure rather than determined attempts to transform the whole nature of the enterprise. The dominant mode of historical writing in Wales at the turn of the century makes the point well. Owen M. Edwards stressed that the two great ages of Welsh history had been the age of the princes and the present age of the people. It took some imagination to reconcile them but the Tudors provided the necessary magic wand. As Lloyd George pointed out, the British Empire had been founded by a Welshwoman (Elizabeth the First, if help is needed in identification!) and his companion in Cymru Fydd, Tom Ellis, liked to celebrate the destiny of the Welsh within the British Empire. Edwards's great medieval hero was not the Llywelyn ap Gruffydd that modern Welsh nationalists like to celebrate, with his sticky and treacherous end at Irfon Bridge in 1282, but his now largely disregarded grandfather Llywelyn ap Iorwerth who had made his state within the framework of the British polity. He was obviously the decent Welsh liberal that his grandson failed to be! Welsh history was a triumphal progress, something most graphically illustrated in the negotiations for the Irish Treaty in 1921. Eamon De Valera enshrined the dominant Irish view that history led nowhere; it was an unending struggle between Brits and Irish and past and present dissolved into each other. He infuriated Lloyd George by wanting to talk about Cromwell, when Lloyd George wanted to discuss present details. In Wales the harmonious development of its history was stressed; there may have been conflicts in the past, but the present was one of beneficent harmony. A particularly nauseous example comes from the investiture of 1911. Dr. J Lynn Thomas observed:

The pulse of Wales has for generations been steadily beating with loyalty to the English crown...The spirits of the departed Welsh princes and warrior-patriots hovered above the eerie mountain peaks and the smiling hilltops of Wales, with invisible faces turned towards Caernarfon. The phantom in turmoil upon the waters of Cardigan Bay...the inaudible fairy sounds of every glen reminded the living that the past Titans of *Cantref y Gwaleod*, of the lake dwellers and of the *Tylwyth Teg* were flurrying to the present as perplexed on-lookers on the historic gathering- unique in the history of Wales.

Why were the spirits so perplexed? They saw a Welsh-speaking peace-warrior at the gates of Caernarfon Castle receiving and greeting the watchful King, his Queen and their eldest son in the neighbourhood where Wales fought many furious battles and lost her independence and yesterday they witnessed Wales regaining her proud heritage in the constitution of the British Empire.

With shades of night the perlpexed throng of the spirit-world vanished into eternal peace, bearing a strange, glorious, ethereal message- Wales is united.

It had not always been so. The libels of 1847 and the *Times*, opinion of 1866 that 'the Welsh language is the curse of Wales' were still present and much of the frantic respectability of nineteenth century nonconformist Wales can be explained as arguments for recognition of the Welsh within the British family. The respectable image that was manufactured to be sold to the English after 1847 was a means of gaining admitance. Yet underneath the celebration of Wales and the British Empire was a rough edge of cultural conflict, a sense of exclusion, which it was felt that only national mobilisation could resolve. Here is Lloyd George, speaking to the successful Welsh at the Cymmrodorion Society in London in 1908. Listen carefully, and to the interjections of his audience. A small nation was watched more closely, he observed; if an Englishman failed he was 'Smith'; if a Welshman failed, he was not 'Jones' but 'Welshmen'.

But Englishmen were generous, and if they attributed the failure of the Welshman to the defects of his race, they also ascribed his success to the credit of his nationality. Therefore every Welshman who succeeded in any branch added a great deal to the national asset, to the common stock on which they all drew in their way through life. (Cheers). It was a great reserve fund for every Welshman to begin life with. (Hear, hear). Wales was in a period of great struggle. It was getting on, perhaps it had not yet 'arrived'...She was called 'poor little Wales.' Poverty was the best training ground for a nation, for it hardened her, gave her grit, stamina, and fitted her for the better land. He believed the success of Scotsmen was due very largely to the difficulties of their climate (laughter)- coupled of course with the magnificent educational system they had got- (hear, hear)- and the result undoubtedly was that they were at the present moment the strongest race in the British Empire. (Hear, hear) They would not be for long. (Laughter and hear, hear) They had won the regard and confidence of other kindred nationalities. The Scottish accent was almost as good as a testamonial. (Laughter) They would not succeed as Welshmen until they put the Welsh accent in that place.

The Welsh, unlike the Irish, believed that the British state was flexible enough to admit them. Yet they would not accept that state in its pure and undiluted form. Their quest for religious rights was one aspect of the struggle; there were other aspects that they felt needed transformation. When Lloyd George was at Balmoral in 1910 and 1911, he was appalled at what he saw. 'The whole atmosphere reeks with Toryism. I can breathe it & it depresses and sickens me'; not that he was overawed, though he confined his more subversive thoughts to the Welsh language "The King is a very jolly chap *ond diolch i Dduw does dim llawer yn ei ben o.*" [but thank God there isn't much in his head.]

One of the clearest avenues for the expression of Welsh hostility to the English state was in the area of military recruiting. There were constant complaints from the military and from the Tories that Welsh nonconformists were reluctant to join the colours. In 1854, Sir Richard Bulkley denounced opposition to recruiting during the Crimean War, by appealing to nonconformist traditions: 'He reminded the sectarians that Cromwell, though a puritan and a fanatic, had yet the good sense to attend to the defence of his country, the rights of his subjects and the balance of power throughout the world.' In Aberystwyth a man paraded with a placard bearing the cat o' nine tails to remind volunteers of their possible fate in the colours. The same complaints of nonconformist hostility were being made in 1908. Thomas Levi, moderator of the Calvinistic Methodists, observed that the true Christian spirit was anti-militarist. Others were afraid of the corruption of innocent Welsh youth by the wicked Saxon army. These attitudes were not simply the creation of Tory propaganda. In 1843-4 only 167 out of 17,450 recruits to the British army were Welsh-born; in 1913 only 1.36% of the army and 2.4% of that year's recruits were Welsh-born.

The army did little to make itself acceptable to Wales; it held all its ceremonies in Anglican Churches and saw patriotism as a British virtue rather than a Welsh one. Otherwise it stressed regimental loyalties and never saw the possibility of exploiting Welsh national feeling for its ends. This is what Lloyd George, in his full myth-making flights, did in 1914. In order to boost recruiting in the First World War, he constantly referred to Welsh militarism- the heroic resistance to the Saxon, the winning of those great 'English' victories of Crecy and Agincourt by Welsh archers and much more to the same effect. Keith Robbins has recently argued that the response to the First World War shows how successfully integrated British society had become, despite its regional and national diversity. Overall recruiting from Wales was at a lower level per head of population than for England and Scotland, but it is the huge increase in the volume of recruiting compared with the past that is most noticable. The great resistance of the nineteenth-century crumbled in the face of propaganda and moral pressure. People joined up as Welshmen, or as members of local communities rather than as British citizens. A Welsh Army Corps was created at the instigation of Lloyd George. Others were drawn in by the weight of local pressure; in East Denbighshire, the parliamentary recruiting committee, took local censuses of men of military age and then sent local worthies to browbeat them into joining up. The combined influence of Wales and the locality was crucial; the British Empire was remote and intangible and did not have this immediate appeal.

The greatest difficulty for the army, throughout the nineteenth-century and in the war itself was in rural areas. In 1915, in one Denbighshire market town, when the Royal Welsh Fusileers marched in with drums beating and bugles blowing to recruit, the local farmers marched their labourers out at the other end! Others hid their labourers away on the mountains when recruiters were around; some recruiters were threatened with shotguns. In some parts of Wales the British state was much more remote than in others. After the war there were determined efforts to capitalise on that sense of national unity and preserve in the stone of war memorials and in the annual ceremonies around them. Yet still people joined the Empire as members of their local community. In the Vale of Clwyd, the people of Llanbedr refused to contribute to the Rhuthun memorial and insisted on their own, as did several small communities in the area. It was local worlds that had to be mobilised for the war effort, and to commemorate it too.

In the course of the First World War the link between Wales and the British state was confirmed. Increasingly the sense of Welsh national identity was under threat by then. Industrial conflict, errupting in 1910-11 in particular but becoming a feature of the whole period to 1926, was something that dissolved the sense of common purpose in Wales. Tonypandy, as Dai Smith has argued was a symbol of changed social relationships- a remaking of the Welsh working class in which the leadership of middle class Liberals was thrown off. Quickly the political unity of Wales disintegrated. By the 1920s, the Tories held the south Wales coastal belt and Labour was entrenched in the valleys. Liberals were left with the rural remnants. The economic crisis of the interwar period swept a fifth of the Welsh population out of the country; those that remained had relatives in Slough or Coventry rather than in Cardiganshire or Builth Wells. They were becoming integrated into Britain rather than with their rural roots, as had been the case in the past. Religion declined precipitously, as did the language. Most of the bonds that had tied nineteenth century Wales together did not survive the crisis of European society of 1910-20, and it fragmented into its constituent parts.

Even before the war there were signs of this, when triumphant Liberalism had tried to give Wales its national institutions. Their location was a matter of bitter dispute, and in the end they were split between Cardiganshire and Cardiff. Other parts of Wales thought they had a claim too. Already, before the war, this had become a bitter issue. In 1913 the Welsh National Memorial Association decided to move its offices from Newtown to Cardiff. There were howls of anguish from all over rural Wales when the news was announced- not just from the affected area, which might be expected- but from areas which identified with its plight. The *Montgomeryshire Express*, (an enlightened newspaper- when the county decided to build a new asylum rather than refurbish the old one it ran the headline "LUNATICS FIRST- RATEPAYERS SECOND"!) was appalled at Cardiff's "selfish rapacity for national honours" and felt that the transfer of the offices to the south "will prove inimical to the best interests of this great national movement, by reason of the harmony it will endanger". The *Liverpool Daily Post*, elaborated a polycentric theory of nationalism: "The centralisation of all authority in one city is a bad thing for the rest of the country...The more towns there are with national institutions, or with some nerve centre of the national life in them, the better for the country as a whole." A correspondent of the *Montgomeryshire Express*, drew on both Welsh history and racial ideolgies for his views.

There are four ancient provinces of Wales, to wit, Gwynedd, Powys, Deheubarth and Morgannwg: and if a strong united front is not immediately shown by the three less populous provinces, the whole of the national institutions (except the Library) will... be located in Morgannwg- and in one town thereof, namely Chinatown.

What underlay this bitterness was the unevenness of development in Wales. In Newtown in particular (which had already fallen from its great days as the 'Leeds of Wales') there were fears that it would revert to being the village that it had once been. Regional imbalance, like class conflict, was a time bomb ticking away underneath the edifice of Liberal nonconformist Wales.

The emergence of Plaid Cymru in 1925 expressed this disintegration and the ebbing of the old sense of self confidence. History became a sad decline from medieval glories. Welsh culture was only safe if preserved in the aspic of a rural society; they did not try to foster rural development, as Liberalism had done, but to impede it. Too much had been developed in rural Wales, and more change threatened the whole basis of Welsh identity. In 1938 Iorwerth Peate attacked the proposed trunk route between north and south Wales because a country without self government would not be able to preserve its culture in these circumstances. The *Western Mail*, commented acidly that "Mr Peate has worked so long in a museum that he is anxious to see the Welsh intelligence deposited there." That was unfair, but what did emerge was a fortress nationalism which felt that identity could be preserved only in the rural areas.

This creed was especially hostile to the industrial society of the south and the cosmopolitan popular culture which inhabited it. South Wales was linked by its trade unionism into the structure of Britain, and very conscious of itself as an industrial society. But its sense of its own distinctive place in the world was underdeveloped. Its second generation had largely cut loose their moorings. By 1940 Wales was far more divided than it had been in 1900.

How then did modernisation affect Wales, its identity and its integration into the British state? The expanding influence of communications, migratory patterns and industrialisation all well attested and undeniable influences whose power increased steadily. Customary behaviour whithered in their path. So much need not be contested. Modernisation theory, when applied to national consiousness, tends to go beyond this and to posit a once and for all shift from local loyalties and 'traditional' values towards national and rational ones. It is evident that local identities did not disappear though they did shrink in importance. Identity is a resource that people use in their lives and is not something which can be read off simply from geography or economic indicators. It must be seen positively and for its mobilising potential. Recent discussions of the fortunes of Welsh identity in the twentieth century have come to conclusions which stand at polar extremes. Surveying the century since 1880, Ken Morgan has concluded that Welsh identity has steadily increased never been stronger than it is currently. It is more usual for observers to be pessemistic, for the decline of the Welsh language and of religion, those crucial indicators of nineteenth century identity, have seemed to leave a gap which is hard to fill. For Gwyn Williams the crucial votes of 1979- against devolution and with a massive swing to the Tories in the following general election- promises the extinction of Wales as a separate entity not its continuance. If we are to make sense of Welshness it needs to be (I apologise for the ugly word) deconstructed. Ken Morgan is focussing on the range of institutions which have emerged in twentieth-century Wales and for which no parallel can be found in the past. The Welsh Office, Welsh Development Agency, Welsh (National!) Region of the B.B.C. and, more recently, S4C are some of the most visible signs of the phenomenon. In a sense they are the latest manifestation of the trend started in the nineteenth century to assert the place of Wales within the structure of the British state. The analysis of this process is Ken Morgan's forte. Gwyn Williams, as an analyst of Wales's popular struggles, is understandably troubled by the events of the late 70s. The process of change has been such that both can be right in their particular spheres. Wales is no longer as well integrated as a unit as it was in the nineteenth century, and that period represents a historical peak in its development.

The national institutions which have proliferated in twentieth century Wales have many sources, but a major component in their appeal is the leverage which they give to Welsh intellectuals. The British state has proved to be a handy umbrella for their interests. Of course, it has also been a means of achieving something for one of Labour's heartlands. Appeals to the national interests of Wales have served many purposes (and many of them economic) in the long decline of the Welsh economy.

In the nineteenth century, the people of Wales joined Great Britain via the mobilisation of a strong national consciousness. The binding of the country together as a unit served many purposes. It gave an industrialising society roots during the process of change, and the economic prominence of Wales added to its political weight. The economic interests of Wales required the British connection. The working class were absorbed into this alliance after the collapse of their independent aspirations of the 1830s and 40s. Welshness gave them some craved for Victorian respectability, while on the other side of the divide workers' numbers and influence was a necessary part of the coalition, even if that class was sometimes rather worrying. Yet, there was enough nonconformity in that working class, and enough Welsh culture, for the cracks to be more than papered over.

The pressures exerted by modernisation can be responded to in different ways. Circumstances in Ireland made a national mobilisation effective and ultimately led to a national revolution. In Wales a rather different national mobilisation was succeeded by a militant class mobilisation, and one which emphasised the region, and its place in the industrial world rather than the Welsh nation. Popular national mobilisation in the context of integration within the British state made sense in the nineteenth century. Since then it has appealed largely to sections of the Welsh intelligentsia, and they have generally failed to rally broad-based support, outside of Gwynedd. In the process of modernisation, popular national mobilisations have their uses; they also have their time.

THE MODERNISATION OF WALES

JOHN OSMOND

Images - how we imagine ourselves and our future - are extremely important. They relate to aspirations and desires, to the nature of society and how it can be preserved and changed. They are powerful mobilisers of feeling because the speak to people in an emotional way which cannot be understood in terms of reason alone, but has to take into account the world of fantasy as well.

How do we imagine Wales today, let alone in the 1990s or the early part of the 21st Century? What image of Wales as a whole do we have? Do we have any sense of choice about the images that pass through our minds?

Let us consider most immediately a traditional image. Wales's image, or identity if you like, has for much of the 20th century traditionally been defined in terms of economic reliance on farming, coal-mining and steel-making; on non-conformism in religion; and above all on a distinctive language. All these categories have been in such a state of transition in our lifetime that merely to bring the images associated with them up to date is an urgent enough task, without trying to imagine what images might - or should - be our dominant ones in say ten or twenty years.

Though we are still to a large extent imprisoned by the traditional image of Wales we should all be familiar with the statistics that demonstrate it no longer applies. Since World War II employment in farming has fallen to about 2 per cent of those in work in Wales. In the 1950s around 150,000 men were still employed in the south Wales coalfield. Today, following the disastrous 1984-5 strike we have fewer than 4,000 miners working in the coalfield, and the separate area status of South Wales within British Coal's organisation has disappeared. Steel industry employment in Wales peaked at 72,000 in 1970. Now we have fewer than 20,000 men in steel, though the are working modernised integrated plants at Port Talbot and Llanwern

Empty and decaying chapels across Wales testify to the secularisation of a culture, while the language continues its decline - from some 37 per cent speaking Welsh in 1921 to perhaps 18 per cent today.

The question of Wales's self-image was referred to in mid- 1988 in an article in the *Western Mail* by the President of Plaid Cymru, Dafydd Elis Thomas. He wrote:

> Many of Wales' images of itself have in the past been negative. Film-makers, painters, novelists, advertising copy-writers, and poets have all produced a succession of a negative images of Wales. One reason for this is that there does not seem to be such a thing as a coherent national image...(1)

Now this a striking admission for the leader of a nationalist party - with surely a vested interest in a "coherent national image" - to concede. Donald Anderson, the Labour MP for Swansea East and one of the Labour "Gang of Six" that opposed Labour's proposed Assembly in the 1979 Referendum, concluded that the four-to-one 'No' vote:

> ... put a large question mark over whether political institutions can rest on the identity of Wales as a nation. Was the message of the Referendum quite simply that the main loyalty in Wales, in political terms, is to Britain and thereafter to the local community within Wales, rather than Wales itself? (2)

No more dramatic question about Welsh political identity could be posed. And the drama of the question is heightened by the question also being put by the leader of the Nationalist Party that, one might assume, would take the political identity of Wales for granted. In his article Dafydd Elis Thomas goes on to say:

> Parts of Wales always feels the need to vie with each other usually for some goodies to be provided by the British state, or for some incoming industrial project. North versus south divisions, with a "mid" stranded somewhere in between have recently been replaced by more sharp divisions between a Welsh-speaking so-called "heartland", a Valleys, and the rest...(3)

In this essay I want to argue a case: that Wales will only acquire a modern sense of itself fitted to confront the demands and challenges of the 21st century if it somehow acquires a much clearer and more focused sense of identity. I want further to argue that a combination of circumstances, some internal and some external are pushing Wales towards such a recognition, to the creation of such a self-image, if you like. There are, however, powerful obstacles in the way, obstacles bound up with the fragmentation alluded to in that quotation from Dafydd Elis Thomas, and also with the absence of a real notion of Welsh citizenship that can best be demonstrated by comparing Wales with Scotland.

Citizenship is essentially bound up in institutions, and much of Scottish national consciousness is based on the survival, since 1707, of an interlocking institutional framework - in particular, the separate Scottish and legal and education systems and the Scottish Church. Built on the bedrock of the survival of this civil institutional infrastructure have been more political institutions such as the Scottish Office and the Scottish TUC. Of course, we have equivalents in Wales but their history is only recent. The depth and longevity of Scottish institutions has produced a different perception or self-image of identity for the Scots for whom Scottishness has a ring of citizenship about it - a quality that arguably accounted for the narrow "Yes" vote in the 1979 Referendum in Scotland compared with the heavy defeat in Wales.

Alongside this is fragmentation of Welsh sensibility already discussed. What Dafydd Elis Thomas referred to - the Heartland, Valleys and the rest - was the three-Wales model produced by the Aberystwyth political scientist Denis Balsom, based on the 1979 opinion survey by the Welsh Election Study: Y Fro Gymraeg; Welsh Wales (the Valleys); and the rest, British Wales. (4)

A brief look at what can be expected to happen in each area over the coming decade confirms, at least in part, a sense of Wales undergoing increasing fragmentation.

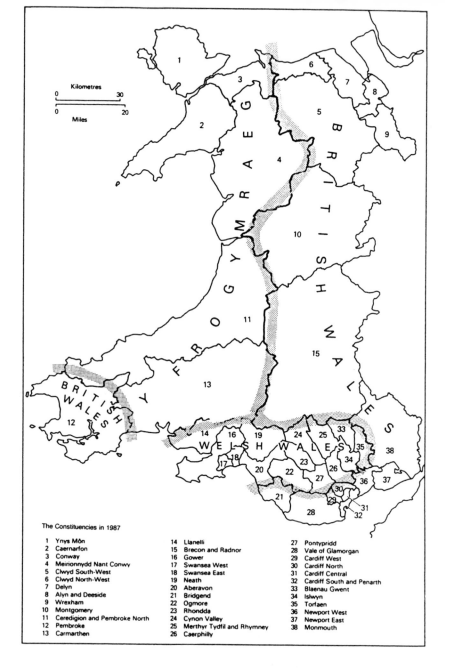

The Constituencies in 1987

1	Ynys Môn	14	Llanelli	27	Pontypridd
2	Caernarfon	15	Brecon and Radnor	28	Vale of Glamorgan
3	Conway	16	Gower	29	Cardiff West
4	Meirionnydd Nant Conwy	17	Swansea West	30	Cardiff North
5	Clwyd South-West	18	Swansea East	31	Cardiff Central
6	Clwyd North-West	19	Neath	32	Cardiff South and Penarth
7	Delyn	20	Aberavon	33	Blaenau Gwent
8	Alyn and Deeside	21	Bridgend	34	Islwyn
9	Wrexham	22	Ogmore	35	Torfaen
10	Montgomery	23	Rhondda	36	Newport West
11	Ceredigion and Pembroke North	24	Cynon Valley	37	Newport East
12	Pembroke	25	Merthyr Tydfil and Rhymney	38	Monmouth
13	Carmarthen	26	Caerphilly		

The Three-Wales Model
(reproduced from John Osmond, (ed) *The National Question Again,*
[Gomer Press, Llandysul, 1985])

Y Fro Gymraeg

This is to a large extent linguistically defined. But though there is no doubt that in this region Plaid Cymru to a large extent sets the political agenda, all four main political groupings have won roughly an equal proportion of the vote. Moreover, it voted as heavily against the projected Assembly in 1979 as anywhere else - though perhaps, there was a distinctive motivation in that many felt their interest would be overwhelmed in an Assembly dominated by the heavily-populated industrialised and anglicised south.

There is a sense of economic and cultural crises in this region that is likely to become more pointed in the years immediately ahead: crises liked to agriculture and in-migration.

About 20 per cent of the population of Gwynedd, Powys and Dyfed have some involvement with agriculture - whether full time or part time. To put this into perspective 19 per cent (or 36,000 people) are employed by local authorities in the area. Nevertheless, farming is extremely important since it underpins the economy Here, the two staples - milk and sheep production, are destined to undergo fundamental decline. The first round of milk quotas in the mid- 1980s cut 2,000 jobs in Welsh farming : and for every 100 jobs lost in milk production another 40 are lost further back in the supply industries. And a "knock forward" effect registers in the servicing and processing industries, as the creamery closures at Llangefni and Felinfach demonstrate.

The only future for Welsh farming is diversification - including greater processing of foods, e.g. soft cheese, and organic production, coupled with the tourist industry dimension. Indigenous farming, however, seems bound to decline even further than it has already during the past generation.

Couple with this in-migration, which achieved a new prominence in Welsh debate as the 1980s drew to a close. Internal migration surveys carried out by the Office of Population, Census and Surveys based on changes in doctors registers - estimated that some 50,000 people were moving into and another 50,000 out of Wales each year. The largest net gains were made by counties in rural Wales. In 1985, for instance, Dyfed gained 2,400 - the highest for any Welsh county.

The impact of these population movements on the indigenous Welsh economy and culture can only be immense. There is hardly a garage, pub or post office in rural Wales that is not owned by an incomer. The schools, especially at primary level are having to cope with an influx that is radically altering the linguistic background of the children.

Welsh Wales - The Valleys

This is Labour's electoral heartland, from which it spread out to dominate Welsh politics for much of this century, and into which it has now to a large extent retreated. The decline and deprivation of the Valley communities - where nearly a third of Wales's 3m people live - is well known. In the early part of this century the Rhondda, for instance, had 66 pits and a population of 185,000. Today it has no pit at all and a population of 85,000. There has been massive emigration, and unlike rural Wales, relatively little in-migration. Those who work often travel outside, to the coastal belt. Housing is among the worst in western Europe. The population that remains is increasingly elderly. The work culture that exists tends to be employee-orientated and lacking in enterprise.

Into this, on the face of it, less than promising context the Welsh Office launched its much-heralded Valleys Initiative in June 1988. There has been much argument about whether the £500m that will be spent under the proposal is new or just recycled money. However, the main point is Peter Walker's claim that it will generate double the amount, around £1 billion in private investment.

Whether it does or not, is more likely to be dependent on the buoyancy of the British economy as a whole over the next few years and that is something outside Peter Walker's control. Nevertheless, as an example of seizing the political high ground within Wales Walker's Valleys initiative was unsurpassed. It is part of a general Conservative project of instilling what is self-consciously termed "the enterprise culture" into Wales, and especially the Valleys where it is seen as specifically lacking.

For instance, in July 1988, the Welsh Schools Inspectors published the results of a survey of Enterprise Education and School Industry Links in 41 secondary schools throughout Wales. This showed that all the schools were now engaged in some form of enterprise education. The Minister of State at the Welsh Office, Wyn Roberts, announced that the enterprise culture was taking root, at last, in Wales. "I believe we are getting a glimpse into the Wales of the future", he declared. (5)

Whatever this means, it certainly implies modernisation. And where the Valleys are concerned who could deny that it is necessary. In terms of political rhetoric, the Conservative administration at the Welsh Office demonstrated during the 1980s greater awareness of and commitment to the need for modernisation than the Opposition parties in Wales.

British Wales

No greater sense and feel of modernisation is to be found than in the remaining region of Wales - British Wales, the coastal belt of south-coast and north-east Wales. Here, for good or ill from the point of view of a distinctive Welsh identity, modernisation has been the name of the game for a generation. The development of new technology industries and the extension of the service sector of the Welsh economy has almost wholly been concentrated in this area. And continued development is assured with ambitious schemes underway for the redevelopment of the river estuaries around Wales - most notably the Cardiff Bay Project, where a £1,700m investment is envisaged during the 1990s. Another barrage is being proposed for the river Usk at Newport - a £40m investment, together with £300m worth of property development as a spin off. Llanelli and Swansea are promoting barrages across their respective estuaries. Not to be outdone Deeside is promoting a £200m Waterfront scheme to be completed by 1993.

Another indication of the economic buoyancy of British Wales was provided in October 1988 when Ford announced Wales' largest ever industrial investment, the £725m extension to its engine plant at Bridgend. This meant the Bridgend plant would spearhead the production of a new range of multi-valve lean-burn engines for the Sierra model of the mid-1990s. It guaranteed the future of the plant into the next century, adding 300 jobs to make a total workforce there of 1,700.

Such developments, of course, serve to enmesh Wales ever more firmly into the international economy. Although control of such investments is far from Wales they are far from London too, and add to the economic arguments for Wales developing a stronger, more autnomous voice within the European Community arena.

Alongside the internationalisation of much of the Welsh economy a parallel trend within the British capitalist system during the 1980s were having the paradoxical effect of putting ownership and control into Welsh-based hands. Such were the effects of the growing number of management buy-outs in Welsh manufacturing industry that began to gather pace from the mid-1980s.

The reason for the growth of the management buy-out phenomenon within the British economy generally are varied but can be narrowed down to three: firstly the change in the political and business climate wrought by the Thatcher years has made ownership a more attractive option for managers previously content to be employees; secondly, the take-over boom of the early 1980s created companies with ill-fitting businesses to sell; and thirdly, bankers, chastened by problems with Third World loans, were seeking safer investment opportunities closer to home. In Wales, however, there was an additional factor at work. Just because Wales has a larger proportion of branch factories, the opportunity for management buy-outs is disproportionately high.

Up-to-date statistics are hard to come by. The only full analysis of the ownership and control of Welsh industry was undertaken by the Welsh Office -nominated Welsh Council in the early 1970s. This found that of Welsh firms employing between 500 and 1,000 people, 78 were controlled from outside and 16 from inside Wales. Of those employing more than 1,000 people, 42 were controlled from outside and only seven from inside Wales. The broad position has changed little since except that there are indications that many outside-owned firms are becoming the target of locally-based buy-outs by managements intent on self-preservation.

A case in point was Plastic Engineers at Treforest in Mid Glamorgan. This was a buy-out from Birmid Qualcast plc in the summer of 1987. It was part of Birmid's engineering division which was being cast adrift in favour of concentrating on consumer durables. Initial funding for Plastic Engineers' buy-out totalled £1.7m - £100,000 coming from the management; £800,000 put in by the 3is investment group; a £600,000 overdraft facility from Barclays Bank; and some support from the Welsh Office. "Our motivation in the buy-out was pure survival", said Plastic Engineers' Chairman Ted Clifforth. "The key to our success since has been shortened, autonomous decision lines and being able to give a personal commitment to our customers". In the year following the buy-out there was a further investment of £1.5m by 3is, the turn-over rose from £4m to £10.5m and the staff increased from 120 to 250. The company also opened a subsidiary in Scotland.

Plastic Engineers are typical of the kind of buy-outs happening in Wales in the late 1980s, both in its scale and the financial investment involved. Between 1985 and 1989 (before which buy-outs were virtually unknown in Wales) there have been an estimated 40 buy-outs of this kind in Wales involving a total investment of around £40m.

It seems likely that a similar level of activity will continue into the 1990s. For instance, the Welsh Venture Capital Fund, a branch of the Welsh Development Agency, was founded in 1985 with £5.5m capital raised from pension funds, Lazards, the Church in Wales, the Welsh Counties, and the Welsh Develpment Agency itself. By mid-1988 it had invested £4m, with £1.3m going into management buy-out ventures. Towards the end of 1988 the Fund was raising a second capital issue, targeted at £10m.

Firms run by local managements bring advantages in a number of distinct ways: they are less likely to be closed at the first hint of recession than outside-owned firms; they attract more research and development opportunities to Wales, and they are more likely to be successful and expand, achieving the much yearned for economic "growth from within". As well as all this they are likely to have a commitment to the Welsh community in a more general sense, for example by funding the arts and community ventures.

So, even in British Wales where Welsh identity is most contested, there are signs of Welsh industry on the one hand having to come to terms more directly with the international economy, focused especially through Brussels, and on the other becoming more Welsh through being owned and controlled from a home base.

What is being discussed here, however, is potential acculturation on a massive scale, as the M4 and A55 respectively bring England into Wales, setting up perhaps a new East/West Divide within Wales to challenge what has previously been perceived as a more fundamental Divide between North and South. Where does the M4 end? If you believe the advertisements in the London papers promoted by Llanelli Borough Council the answer is clear.

The Dynamic of Institutions (6)

However, at least three political developments point in a more hopeful direction so far as the future integrity of Wales is concerned. The first is the continued development of Welsh based institutions. And here there is something of a paradox, pointed up by Dennis Balsom, the author of the Three Wales model we've been discussing:

> The logic of modernisation and development inevitably leads to standardisation and acculturation. In one field only does the Welsh dimension loom large in British Wales: the growth of the government bureaucratic machine in Cardiff. Herein lies the greatest paradox. The institutions that were created in response to particular Welsh demands now largely supervise and oversee the demise of much of the particular character of Wales. Wales, however, remains the rationale of the bureaucratic machine and, what is more, it continues to acquire power and influence rather than to wither like its host. (7)

It might have been thought that, as a consequence of the 1979 referendum, the process of establishing new national institutions and extending the role of the Welsh Office, would be drawn to a close. In fact, the reverse has occurred. Not only have both processes gained a new dynamic, but an entirely new dimension has been added as post-1979 Secretaries of State for Wales have demonstrated a new commitment to promoting industrial regeneration in Wales. Post-1979 Wales has been marked by three related developments entailing the establishment of new

82

national institutions, extending the responsibilities of the Welsh Office, and the creation of distinct strategies by Welsh Office Ministers aimed at securing economic regeneration.

In terms of the creation of new national institutions, 1979 inaugurated a phase of accentuated development, involving initially the establishment of S4C (the Welsh Fourth Channel), followed by a national body to oversee Welsh medium education (though as yet this body lacks funding) and all-Wales bodies to promote health education and sites of historical interest. Another four national institutions were established towards the end of the 1980s: a National Curriculum Council; a Welsh Committee of the UK University Funding Council: a New Welsh Housing Corporation-Tai Cymru; and a Welsh Language Board to promote the status of the language.

Within the Welsh Office and its related institutions similar processes of development were underway. The most important occurred in the immediate wake of the referendum with the Welsh Office securing responsibility of a block grant for its expenditure responsibilities which it negotiates each year directly with the Treasury, the Secretary of State for Wales empowered if necessary to argue his case in Cabinet. The Welsh Office now allocates the block grant between its many areas of responsibility, ranging from education and housing to roads, agriculture and economic development. In particular, it is responsible for distributing central government support - currently in the form of Rate Support Grant - to the eight Welsh counties and 37 districts. The forum where this last process is argued through each year is the Welsh Consultative Committee on Local Government Finance.

Meanwhile the Welsh Development Agency was elaborated through the establishment of WIN vest (transformed in early 1989 into Welsh Development International), to attract inward investment into Wales, and WIN tech, to promote technological development within Welsh industry. Three further ventures involving public sector initiative and participation, were established in the financial and business technology arenas. Hafren Investment Finance was established as a subsidiary to the WDA in 1982, whilst Welsh Development Capital (Management) was set up as a joint venture between the WDA and the Development Capital

Group in January 1985 - both initiatives being attempts to cater for the financial needs of Welsh industry. In July 1988 the Institute of Industrial Technology was established by the WDA at Swansea's Innovation centre. With an initial budget of £380,000 provided jointly by the WDA and Welsh business the Institute aims to help Welsh Industry become more competitive and profitable through the use of computer-controlled manufacturing techniques. Alongside this the WDA simultaneously established the Welsh Technology Fund to provide early-stage high risk financial support for developing innovative ideas. Companies are able to receive funding of up to 50 per cent of a project, up to a maximum of £150,000.

With this economic administrative infrastructure in place the key development in post 1979 Wales has been development of strategies aimed at promoting autonomous Welsh economic regeneration. For Nicholas Edwards this entailed a commitment to use the Welsh Office to establish links between industry, the venture capital market and the University of Wales, with the WDA maintaining a supportive role. After the 1987 General Election Peter Walker maintained this approach It is clear, for example that his insistence that a separate Welsh Committee of the New University Funding Council be established was part of this strategy to secure economic regeneration. Another instance is the enhanced role that has been given the Wales Office of the Overseas Trade Board. Similarly, the marketing of Welsh Crafts is being revamped and integrated on the basis of a stronger Welsh identity. The Welsh Development Agency is leading moves to boost the image of Welsh branded food products.

The main thrust, however, being carried by the targeting of resources on the Cardiff Bay Development Project, initiated by Nicholas Edwards, now followed by Peter Walker's Valleys initiative. These diverse examples illustrate the commitment of the Welsh Office administration in the 1980s (and likely to be carried on into the 1990's) to concerted political intervention in the Welsh economy. This is doubly significant in that it has happened under the umbrella of an overall Conservative administration preferring on the whole to withdraw from intervention in the economy, allowing industry to be left to the cold (and assumed invigorating) draughts of market force. In Wales, however, the presence and continued development of network of administrative institutions, coupled with drive of successive Secretaries of State has secured an interventionist approach.

There is now a very large bureaucratic state structure in existence. The Welsh Office employs around 2,300 civil servants with a further 1,500 in subordinate national institutions. In the 1988-89 financial year, these administered a budget of around £3,500 million, a figure that represented some 80 per cent of public expenditure in Wales (the rest comprising spending on law and order, social security, defence overseas services and debt interest)

The Welsh Office has now charge of the commanding heights of the Welsh economy and society and under its present political control is pursuing a strongly interventionist direction. All this is happening in the absence of effective democratic debate, scrutiny or accountability In the absence of a directly elected Welsh assembly there is simply no mechanism through which democratic control can be exercised.

This position has presented the forces of opposition in Wales with an acute dilemma. Despite being in a minority in Wales, and despite operating on the basis of a non-democratic structure, the Conservatives in Wales have seized the initiative using an interventionist approach to the economy more commonly associated with the left than the right. This has caught opposition politicians off balance, unsure how to respond, and more often than not reduced to carping criticisms of an interventionist economic policy that is securing greater prosperity for the wealthier sections of the Welsh population, overwhelmingly located in the urban centres of coastal south Wales. Over ten, and perhaps 20 years, Conservative administration at the Welsh Office are being given a free hand to remodel Wales according to the dictates of a market-orientated private capitalist ethic. Key community institutions, most notably the health service, and the services administered by local government - education and housing to name only the most important - are taking a back-seat (and in some cases being dismantled) while expenditure priorities forge ahead in other directions. The full significance of the failure of achieving an Assembly in 1979 can now be seen as allowing control of the Welsh Office to fall into the hands of a Conservative administration.

The Wider Context

The development of a Welsh institutional infrastructure - albeit of a bureaucratic rather than democratic character - is not happening in isolation. There is a developing polarity in British culture, economics and. politics between the South-east of Britain and the Northwest - defined by that old historical divide between lowland and upland Britain, the Roman Fosse Way, roughly the line from the Severn to the Wash. Arguably this is likely to have the effect of making Wales as an integral unit more aware of itself, particularly seen within the European framework. Of course, such outside influences do not just apply to Wales. Scotland remains a potentially potent focus for change. A Scottish assembly is firmly on the agenda - indeed has never been off it since 1979, when 52 per cent of those voting said "Yes". What is less appreciated is the change that is occurring in the North of England.

In January 1988 the Northern Group of Labour MPs - mainly from Northumberland, Durham and Cleveland - published a Bill in the House of Commons canvassing the need for a Northern Regional Assembly and a Northern Development agency. This was produced at the same time as the Scottish group of Labour MPs presented a Bill for a Scottish Assembly and signalled a new era of co-operation between the two groups. In the 1970s Northern MPs had vigorously opposed Scottish devolution, fearing it would give Scotland an unfair advantage in the distribution of Treasury resources within the United Kingdom. But in the Autumn of 1987 the Northern and Scottish Groups of Labour MPs hammered out a joint approach. Between them these groups have 75 MPs within the Labour Parliamentary Party making them a powerful bloc.

Binding them together is a growing appreciation of the inequitable distribution of resources and power favouring the South-east within Britain. During the 1980s regional economic policy - which in previous decades did something to offset the concentration of resources in South-east England - was to all intents and purposes axed. Expenditure on regional economic policy in the UK was halved between 1979 to 1986, cut by £1,000m, and was halved again by the end of the decade.

At the same time as regional economic policy was being cut back, defence expenditure increased by nearly 30 per cent between 1979 to 1986. The equipment budget of the Ministry of Defence alone amounted to some £8.3 billion in 1985- 1986. This accounted for half the output of the aerospace and 20 per cent of the electronics industries in Britain, an enormous number of jobs - especially those in research and development establishments.

But the geographical spread of this spending is the most sobering reality so far as the Welsh economy was concerned: England, south of a line drawn from the Severn to the Wash accounted for 68 per cent of it (the South-West 11 per cent, East Anglia 3 per cent, and the south-east a staggering 54 per cent). The Midlands received 9 per cent; the North of England 15 per cent; Scotland 6 per cent; and Northern Ireland and Wales came bottom of the pile with just 1 per cent each. The Ministry of Defence budget is, in practice, an unofficial regional economic policy - working to the advantage of the South-East of England. (8)

The point about these realities, so far as the image or identity of Wales referred to at the opening is concerned, is that a sense of the integrity of Wales is being reinforced by regional differentiations within England. We should not lose sight either of the moves towards integration within the European Community, with the timetable set for the creation of a single market between member states by 1992.

So the modernisation of Wales through the 1990s presents us with what should be by now, customary contradictions. On the one hand we face a growing fragmentation between and within the three Wales discussed above. Yet in parallel with this are forces - a growing internal government bureaucracy, combined with the outside pressures just described - that are giving a greater coherence to the integrity of Wales as a whole.

Imagining Different Futures.

In the leading article of the August 1988 issue of *Planet* magazine its editor, Ned Thomas, made a memorable attack on the policies and attitudes of the President of Plaid Cymru, Dafydd Elis Thomas. Part of the focus for the attack was Elis Thomas's *Western Mail* article about Wales's image quoted near the beginning of this essay. The argument was over that vexed issue of in-migration and the response to it that is both possible and appropriate. The thrust of Ned Thomas's attack was that Plaid Cymru leader was seeking a Wales, or perhaps recognising the inevitability of a future Wales where the Welsh speaking community would not be the defining essence of Welsh identity and nationhood, but part of the mosaic of the nation "a kind of ethnic substratum".

Questioned on HTV's *Y Byd ar Bedwar* (The World on Four, S4C) current affairs programme in June 1988 Dafydd Elis Thomas declared, "I am the president of a national party which reflects the nation as it is". Ned Thomas concludes that this statement implies that not only are there two languages in Wales, but two national cultures and indeed a third immigrant English culture that together make up the nation. He goes on to say that Dafydd Elis Thomas is attempting the impossible in trying to reflect them all.

Ned Thomas reveals his hand, however, when he stresses through the editorial that there can be no sense of territorial belonging in Wales without the language and the sense that it has a firm territorial base. He describes English- speaking Wales as a "frontierless culture". Speaking of the Valleys, for instance he says:

> It is possible to allow the uniqueness of Valleys culture and yet wonder whether in modern conditions and in the English language it is possible for it to transform itself while yet, in some sense, maintaining a "Welsh" character, a continuity of some kind. (9)

This is the nub of the argument. But Ned Thomas ignores a number of powerful elements which guide the sensibility of the English-speaking Welsh: primarily a sense of responsibility for their communities, but beyond that other factors like identification with a landscape, and a growing structure of institutions that above all else, and as argued earlier, define the territory of Wales.

For people like Ned Thomas the Welsh Language is the essence of what makes Wales a distinctive identity. Without it, in fact, Wales could not exist in the way he and others like him think it is or, rather, imagine it should be. Dafydd Elis Thomas, on the other hand, has been struggling to come to terms, and to make his party come to terms, with the reality that in present day Wales, and even more in any future Wales, the language will be one dimension but not the whole of what makes us what we are.

Imagining futures is an especially Welsh preoccupation. It has something to do with our having such a contested past and fraught present. However it is defined, being Welsh is a process of struggle. But through struggle there is life and hope. Towards the end of his panoramic history of the Welsh, *When was Wales?* Gwyn A. Williams reflected:

> The Welsh as a people have lived by making and remaking themselves in generation after generation, usually against the odds, usually within a British context. Wales is an artefact which the Welsh produce. If they want to. It requires an act of choice... (10)

The act of choice is still being made, though not in ways that some in Wales would like. The modern Wales of the 21st Century will be one whose territory is more defined by the institutions that govern it than by a separate language. Hopefully, too, it will be defined by its sense of a relationship with Europe as a whole than just Britain.

In all this there will be some gains and some losses. The language will have to survive in a milieu that is more and more penetrated with English. Yet at the same time, and paradoxically, the British dimension of Welsh identity shall diminish in favour of a European one. Wales may become more like Scotland in that a sense of Welsh citizenship nascent in the Welsh institutions that are continuing to develop could become more pronounced. Whichever way these questions are resolved, Wales will modernise. As the 20th Century draws to a close, the people of Wales are beginning to catch up with a process that is happening to some extent in spite of themselves.

NOTES

(1) Dafydd Elis Thomas, "Ridding Wales of a Siege Mentality" *Western Mail*, 9th July 1988.

(2) Donald Anderson, "Reconciling Socialism with Community" in John Osmond (ed) *The National Question Again - Welsh Political Identity in the 1980's* (Llandysul, 1985). p.176-7.

(3) Dafydd Elis Thomas "Ridding Wales...".

(4) See Dennis Balsom, "The Three Wales Model" in John Osmond ed) *The National Question Again*.

(5) *Western Mail*, 1 July 1988.

(6) For some of the information in this section I am indebted to the work of Emyr Williams. See particularly his discussion paper "The Welsh Senate and the Regeneration of Wales", Plaid Cymru, 51 Cathedral Road, Cardiff, 1987, and his article "The State without People" in *Planet* 69, June 1988. See also my own more detailed analysis of the theme, *The Dynamic of Institutions in The National Question Again*, as above.

(7) Denis Balsom, "Three Wales Model...", p.16.

(8) See John Osmond, *The Divided Kingdom*, (London, 1988) pp 51-4.

(9) Ned Thomas, "Can Plaid Cymru Survive Until 1994?" in *Planet*, No. 70, August 1988.

(10) Gwyn A Williams, *When was Wales?* (Harmondsworth, 1985), p.304.

Further Reading

Given the range of this occasional paper, it would be impossible to give a full bibliography. What follows is a list of some articles and books that were found to be useful in the writing of the introductory essay, the main texts cited by the contributors, along with one or two items of particular relevance that have appeared recently.

Neal Ascherson, *Games with Shadows*, (London, 1988)

Geoffrey Ashe, (ed.) *The Quest for Arthur's Britain*, (London, 1968)

Theo Barker, "Business as Usual? London and the Industrial Revolution" *History Today*, February, 1989

Jim Bulpitt, *Territory and Power in the United Kingdom: An Interpretation*, (Manchester, 1983)

Geoffrey Bell, *The Protestants of Ulster*, (London, 1976)

Terence Brown, *Ireland: A Social and Cultural History, 1922-79*, (London, 1981)

Steve Bruce, *God Save Ulster! The Religion and Politics of Paisleyism*, (Oxford, 1987)

David Cannadine, "The Context, Performance and Meaning of Ritual: The British Monarchy and the 'Invention of Tradition', c.1820-1977" in Eric Hobsbawm and Terence Ranger (eds) *The Invention of Tradition*, (Cambridge, 1983)

David Cannadine, "Victoria" in David Herman,(ed.) *Late Great Britons*, (Brook Production/ B.B.C. 1988)

Kenneth Cargill, (ed.) *Scotland 2000*, (Glasgow, 1987)

Linda Colley, "Whose Nation? Class and National Consciousness in Britain, 1750-1830", *Past and Present*, No. 113, November 1986.

Linda Colley, "The Apotheosis of George III: Loyalty, Royalty and the British Nation, 1760-1820", *Past and Present*, No. 102, February 1984.

Robert Colls and Phillip Dodd, (eds) *Englishness: Politics and Culture, 1880-1920*, (London, 1986)

D. Hywel Davies, *A Call to Nationhood: The Welsh Nationalist Party, 1925-1945*, (Cardiff, 1983)

Victor Edward Durkacz, *The Decline of the Celtic Languages: A Study of Linguistic and Cultural Conflict in Scotland, Wales and Ireland from the Reformation to the Twentieth Century*, (Edinburgh, 1983)

Stephen Ellis, "Crown, Community and Government in the English Territories, 1450-1575", *History*, Vol. 71 No. 232 June 1986.

Stephen Ellis, "'Not Mere English': The British Perspective, 1400-1650", *History Today*, December 1988.

Neil Evans, "The Great Game of Britain: The Politics of Identity in a Divided Kingdom", *Planet*, No. 72, December/January 1988-9.

Alan Everitt, "Country, County and Town: Patterns of Regional Evolution in England", *Transactions of the Royal Historical Society*, 5 Ser. Vol. 29 1979.

Samuel E. Finer, "Statebuilding, State Boundaries and Border Control", *Social Science Information*, Vol. 13 1974.

Michael Freeman, "The Industrial Revolution and the Regional Geography of England: A Comment", *Transactions of the Institute of British Geographers*, New Ser. Vol 9 1984.

V.H. Galbraith, "Nationality and Language in Medieval England", *Transactions of the Royal Historical Society*, 4 Ser. Vol. XXIII 1941

Tom Garvin, "Anatomy of a Nationalist Revolution: Ireland, 1858-1928", *Comparative Studies in Society and History*, Vol. 28 No. 3 July 1986.

Ernest Gellner, *Nations and Nationalism*, (Oxford, 1983)

Ralph A. Griffiths, *"This Royal Throne of Kings, this Sceptred Isle": The English Realm and Nation in the Later Middle Ages*, (Inaugural Lecture, University College Swansea, 1983)

Elizabeth Hammerton and David Cannadine, "Conflict and Consensus on a Ceremonial Occasion: The Diamond Jubilee in Cambridge, 1897" *Historical Journal*, Vol. 24 No. 1 March 1981.

Christopher Harvie, *Scotland and Nationalism: Scottish Society and Politics, 1707-1977*, (London, 1977)

Christopher Harvie, *Against Metropolis: Socialism and Decentralisation*, (Fabian Tract 484, London, 1982)

Michael Hechter, *Internal Colonialism: The Celtic Fringe in British National Development, 1536-1966*, (London, 1975)

Hugh Kearney, *The British Isles: The History of Four Nations*, (Cambridge, 1989)

Paul Kennedy, *The Rise and Fall of the Great Powers: Economic Change and Military Conflict from 1500 to 2000*, (London, 1988)

Hans Kohn, "The Genesis and Character of English Nationalism", *Journal of the History of Ideas*, Vol. 1 No. 1 January 1940.

John Langton, "The Industrial Revolution and the Regional Geography of England", *Transactions of the Institute of British Geographers*, New Ser Vol. 9 No. 2 1984.

C.H. Lee, "Regional Growth and Structural Change in Victorian Britain", *Economic History Review*, 2 Ser. Vol. 34 No. 3 August 1981.

F.S.L. Lyons, *Culture and Anarchy in Ireland, 1890-1939*, (Oxford, 1979)

Colin MacCabe, "Death of a Nation: Television in the Early Sixties", *Critical Quarterly*, Vol. 20 No. 2 Summer 1988.

Oliver MacDonagh, *Ireland: The Union and its Aftermath*, (2nd ed. London 1977)
Oliver MacDonagh, *States of Mind: A Study of Anglo-Irish Conflict, 1780-1980*, (London, 1983)

Hugh A. MacDougall, *Racial Myth in English History: Trojans, Teutons and Anglo-Saxons*, (Montreal/ Hanover New Hants, 1982)

David Miller, *Queen's Rebels: Ulster Loyalism in Historical Perspective*, (Dublin, 1978)

Kenneth O. Morgan, *Wales in British Politics, 1868-1922*, (Cardiff, 1963)

Kenneth O. Morgan, *Rebirth of a Nation: Wales, 1880-1980*, (Oxford and Cardiff, 1981)

Kevin Morgan, "Regional Regeneration in Britain: The Territorial Imperative and the Conservative State", *Political Studies*, Vol. XXXIII No. 4 December 1985.

John Morrill, *The Revolt of the Provinces: Reactions to the English Civil War, 1630-50*, (2nd ed. London, 1980)

Tom Nairn, *The Break-up of Britain: Crisis and Neo-Nationalism*, (2nd ed. London 1981)

Tom Nairn, *The Enchanted Glass: Britain and its Monarchy*, (London, 1988)

John Osmond, (ed.) *The National Question Again: Welsh Political Identity in the 1980s*, (Llandysul, 1985)

John Osmond, *The Divided Kingdom*, (London, 1988)

Alan Butt Philip, *The Welsh Question: Nationalism in Welsh Politics, 1945-1970*, (Cardiff, 1975)

Keith Robbins, *Core and Periphery in Modern British History*, (London, British Academy, Raleigh Lecture on History, 1985)

Keith Robbins, *Nineteenth-Century Britain: Integration and Diversity*, (Oxford, 1988)

Keith Robbins, "North and South: Then and Now", *History Today*, April 1988.

Brian Robson, "Coming Full Circle: London versus the Rest, 1890-1980" in George Gordon, (ed.) *Regional Cities in the U,K,, 1890-1980*, (London, 1985)

Ivan Roots, "Union and Disunion in the British Isles, 1637-1660" in Roots, (ed.) *"Into Another Mould": Aspects of the Interregnum*, (Exeter, 1981)

Richard Rose, *Understanding the United Kingdom: The Territorial Dimension in Government*, (London, 1982)

Conrad Russell, "The British Problem and the English Civil War", *History*, Vol. 72 No. 236 October 1987.

W. D. Rubinstein, "Wealth, Elites and the Class Structure of Modern Britain", *Past and Present*, No. 76 August, 1977.

Francis Sheppard, "London and the Nation in the Nineteenth Century", *Transactions of the Royal Historical Society*, 5th Ser. Vol. 35 1985.

Dai Smith, *Wales! Wales?* (London, 1984)

Christopher Smout, "Centre and Periphery in History; with Some Thoughts on Scotland as a Case Study", *Journal of Common Market Studies*, Vol. XVIII No. 3 March 1980.

Michael Steed, "The Core-Periphery Dimension of British Politics", *Political Geography Quarterly*, Vol. 5 No. 4 October 1986.

A.T.Q. Stewart, *The Narrow Ground: Aspects of Ulster 1609-1969*, (London, 1977)

Lawrence Stone, "The Reformation", in his, *The Past and the Present Revisited*, (London, 1987)

Humphrey R. Southall, "The Origins of the Depressed Areas: Unemployment, Growth and Regional Economic Structure in Britain before 1914", *Economic History Review*, 2 Ser. Vol. 41 No. 2 May 1988.

Keith Thomas, "The United Kingdom" in Raymond Grew, (ed.) *Crises of Political Development in Europe and the United States*, (Princeton, 1978)

David Vincent, "Communication, Community and the State" in Clive Emsley and James Walvin (eds) *Artisans, Peasants and Proletarians, 1760-1860: Essays Presented to Gwyn Williams*, (London, 1985)

Gwyn A. Williams, *When Was Wales? A History of the Welsh*, (London, 1985)

Aristide R. Zolberg, "Strategic Interventions and the Formation of Modern States: France and England", *International Social Science Journal*, Vol. XXXII No. 4 1980.